# pimp

SHASHANK GUPTA

tara
India Research Press

PIMP

*Shashank Gupta*

tara
India Research Press
Flat 6, Khan Market, New Delhi - 110003
Ph: 24694610; Fax : 24618637
www.indiaresearchpress.com
contact@indiaresearchpress.com

**2015**



ISBN 13 : 978-81-8386-130-4
ISBN 10 : 81-8386-130-X



Printed for Tara-India Research Press at *Manipal Technologies Limited.*

*This book is for you,*
*Priyanka Choudhary.*

# *Chapter 1*

I am a seventy-year-old pimp. If you must still go on, let's flashback ten years to Chapter 2, my first jottings.

I said turn the page, Moron.

# *Chapter 2*

It felt like I was fired from a canon. I worked at this really nice charity factory for the blind for forty years, and then made a silly mistake for which they asked me to shove off. I turned sixty.

So naturally, I went lost in all the time I couldn't fill and wandered off to the sea, a walk away from my house, every morning. You only had to go over a slope and there it was, the heaving bosom, inviting you to drown. Emarti said she saw me talking to a bougainvillea at the promenade, but that was merely her miserable attempt at controlling my mind after all these years. Wives are witches, every dog knows; their skulls are pots where some stew is forever steaming and you are made to feel an important ingredient. And wives generally have rather long lives.

That day, I was watering the mentioned shrub as usual, I wasn't talking to it. I have these huge glasses of melon juice before I venture out and the sight of the bougainvillea makes me want to pee.

Now, when I pulled the zipper up, I yelped hell. I could well imagine how a grown-up's circumcision feels, why everything goes whiteout in the movies when the hero takes a hit. I saw my life freefall from sixty to zero in two seconds. There was blood all over my trouser-front.

There were guttural pigeons eating and painting everything dirty white. There were two million oblivious couples trying to make-out on the rocks. There was a girl with sweaty armpits walking towards me, pretending to be alarmed.

"It's nothing," I tried shooing her away from the distance, "go back to your lover or whatever."

"He didn't turn up," she was looking around angrily. She said 'blood' as if she meant 'ketchup'.

I had to nod. She didn't start screaming or anything, just sat down on the parapet with her hand to her mouth to stifle a cry or muffle a laugh, I'll never know. I left her to her emotions and tried working the zipper again.

"Oh, Bitch!" I cried out. The girl came running. She had no idea she was about to change my life forever. Her fingers held the crocodile jaws of my pants and, as if she'd been doing this all her ugly life, with one swift jerk freed me from its bite. How I wished her sweat smelt sweeter.

"How can I thank you," I didn't ask her, just said it as small talk.

"You can invite us to your house."

"Eh?"

"You can invite us to your house."

"Us?" Suddenly my tongue took refuge in dwarf sentences.

"My friend and I. I'm sure you live close by."

A puny fellow had arrived and was now beaming over her shoulder. A quick look informed me he was made of inferior parents and most probably wore a body odour imitating prawns drying on the beach.

"Why?" I wanted to know.

He spoke out of turn, "Because, Uncle, these rocks are sorely hard and we need a room to ourselves for an hour." He was laughing so uncontrollably that my next bark knocked his eyes out.

"Okay," said I, beginning to lead the way. I heard a lot of nervous whispering behind my back. I was certain they were nudging each other in the nipples.

"Uncle," the girl called out, "you can charge us by the hour." I was completely smitten by her honesty.

Emarti met us at the first landing. I didn't waste time explaining to her that the house was mine and I won't allow her to discourage visitors. Her face contorted sideways, her eyes went wide, her lips twitched like dying fish and she made sounds of a horse snorting after a short run. She looked so funny I laughed into my handkerchief and pushed the two lovers into one of the ten extra rooms my father built.

I was always allergic to the house. The moment I entered, I would sneeze. Ten times, twenty times and sometimes late into the night. The doctors tested randomly for things as unsuspecting as bird-droppings and came out tossing their heads like asses chasing away a filthy thought. But it was on the day Emarti went away for an anal surgery or worse that I made the great connect. My allergen was a peculiar pineapple odour, and it emanated from a living breathing being: Emarti.

Stubbornly, she refused to sleep in a different room, so I took my stuff to the second floor. My father was not a fool when he built such a big house for three people. And at that moment, in one of the spare rooms, his vision was beginning to make sense.

I sat on the stairs, should Emarti become too nosey. Everything suddenly seemed to fall into place. I had been in the blind school business all my life and it was natural to start my own shop. There is no real difference in caring for children without eyes or couples without a roof for a few hours. Both are needy. Both are helpless. Both were nothing without money and managers.

I glanced at my watch and rapped on the door. "One hour up," I tried to be as discreet as I could.

Emarti's head popped out of the kitchen and she watched me with angry, slit-thin eyes. Unaffected, I knocked on the door again.

"Coming, Uncle," the boy sounded annoyed.

"Hurry up, I haven't all July," I lied.

"Coming, Uncle," cried the girl this time.

I sat down. In the school for the blind you can't be too kind. My mind was running hazy, framing rules, because word would go around and I couldn't be caught with my zipper down. Not in the business sense, at least. These two had to be told that the morning favour had been paid for and the metre was running big time. No exceptions.

The door opened. I pretended not to notice any change in their appearances, though I had to acknowledge a new smell that had walked out with them. They descended a couple of steps when the girl turned sweetly and said, "Thank you."

I think I smiled the entrepreneur smile.

"By the way, Uncle," she smiled back, "what will be the charge, if someone was to ask?"

I knew I was on my way.

# *Chapter 3*

My inflamed foreskin was a pain. Had I been a snake, I would have shed it near the bougainvillea. Peeing in public spaces became a sin. I stopped drinking water and melons were banned at the house. I remembered reading somewhere of how a reptile's bite kills by filling the wound with deadly living bacteria. My own crocodile had such rusty teeth, I saw myself losing my new business to antiseptics before it had hardly begun. How many desperate lovers had been turned away from the door! I could see Emarti grinning through her asphyxiation-blue lipstick. Our still-born affection, it must be amply clear by now, had long turned smelly and begged a speedy burial. Had she not been someone's parting gift, I would not have suffered her charm beyond the third year. All I could do was wait for her to make the one big mistake every man longs for: honesty spelt out.

On the thirteenth day, I went for my walk again. Nothing happened, no one followed me home. More than money, my mind was losing my patience. I strode down to the sea-face the next morning, no longer angry with the world. Blind men have to be shown the way once, for them to follow blindly.

A car was parked precariously close to a tree. You couldn't open the passenger door even if you wanted to, which meant the occupants were still inside instead of lounging on the rocks. I tapped on the glass. No response. I tapped again. The darkened glass slid down a chink.

"What!" he demanded.

Putting my fingers between the glass and the car, lest he shut me out, I came to the point, "I see you want a room."

"Get lost."

"A room for two hours." Whispering began within the car and went on to become a hissing, much to my impatience. "Want it or not?"

"Give us a second, Uncle," the angry man of a minute ago had become a relation in a matter of four words. Much to my annoyance, this 'uncle' thing was starting to stick to me. I didn't know then how very soon it would become my working title in the circuit.

The man rolled down the glass, "Where do we go?"

When I slipped into the backseat, it dawned on me this was a rich man's car and he would have a house larger than mine, but not the room he was looking for. The bigness of my idea slapped me repeatedly. I smiled to myself.

"You don't look the type," my client was saying.

"You don't look the type either," said I.

"Mind your mouth."

"You are some beggar. I'll get off here." A long silence ensued. Neither did he stop driving nor did I jump out. I learnt something new: I was fast losing respect, which was good for my peace. All virginal virtues - honesty, responsibility, kindness, wisdom, trust - added up to the respect a person earned in his lifetime. But these also bound him to a suffocating cage he could not leave. A man with a 'reputation' is not bothered by scruples, not burned under the magnifying gaze of society - he is free. Has little to lose.

My first ever payment was a bitch. The girl who stepped out of the car was barely there. She was filthy, drugged and the man just left her on the bed and walked away after shoving me the cash. I kept it pressed in a diary to remind me of certain things I had told myself then. When you handle blind people, you have to have x-ray eyes.

She wore rags. I waited till midnight for want of a way. And then called for a cab to take us to the hospital - the only place where no one cares who you are carrying. Pretending to go check on the doctor, I escaped leaving her grumbling to herself on a wheelchair. Once back behind my doors I laughed myself into a cough.

"Quality, Uncle, quality," I wiped my tears, "don't ever forget quality."

That girl also happened to be twelve and no more.

# Chapter 4

Some people have all the luck. I was plucking it off a cherry tree, eating it, juicing it, pickling it and even hitting passers-by with it. Wealth was merely the kernel, a by-product of the equation. The house was running full of affection between ten in the morning and ten in the night. I had devised a way of managing traffic so no one ran into anyone who was someone you knew. I simply locked the rooms from outside and when there was a knock, I let the occupants out. The flow of couples was always in the clockwise direction, inspired by airports.

All this happened very fast, I had no idea I would soon be turning applicants away. It did occur to me to purchase the neighbour's house, but they had stopped talking to me for reasons I did not enquire into; and I'm not the type who tries to pry under the surface. Real beauty is skin deep, deep down we are all bastards.

I felt like heaven.

Dark clouds were beginning to gather.

I had an unexpected visit.

Sometime late after midnight, the phone jangled. Before I could stir, Emarti held the receiver. She had altogether stopped sleeping weeks ago; this sudden change in her demeanour warned and excited me. She no longer howled at the doorbell; hers was a silence contained in a cleaver. I think I had finally disturbed her squeaky-clean life and my reading was that anything could happen. I had gone and hurt her religion. Her big mistake was probably just about to be committed.

The caller must have asked, "Uncle?"

Emarti replied, "No, I'm not your Uncle. He's in here somewhere, waiting to die."

To which he would have said something ugly.

And Emarti banged the phone down with a very dirty word for his mother, after telling him, "Yeah sure, you go ahead and try. Uncle will personally slaughter you in broad daylight." This unannounced respect for me was so unlike her. I tried to smell the rat between the lines.

Within minutes the door rang furiously.

I am not the kind to be rattled by bells, however big. In fact, I enjoy noise so much that I let the ringing go on for a while. It was only when my glass windows started shattering, I feared the law and opened the door to a couple of boys almost twenty.

"You're Uncle?" They spoke together.

"You broke my window?"

"You have a wife?"

"Are you hired killers?" I voiced my hunch without mincing emotions. They were asking stupid things to be sure of the address.

"Was she the one on the phone?"

"Aren't you mad she called your mother a dry cow's udder?"

"You want her to die too, don't you?" the shorter one half-laughed. I was about to open my mouth when I saw her standing there with a screwdriver pointing at me. That altered the mood a bit. She wouldn't have stuck the tool into my gut, of course, she was merely indicating the target and underlining the contract with it. What she'd barked on the phone was a signal to them that I was home.

"Have you been troubling her lately?" said the other.

"Did she hire you two, you bull's genitalia?" I spoke with fully-grown certainty.

"What do you think?"

"What if I doubled what she promised you?" I asked, keen on making most of this opportunity to finally rid myself of Emarti with least sweat. I steadied my pounding brain by clenching my jaws. It made me look fierce and disguised my hope.

"Do you think we have no honour?"

"Do you think I have no money?"

"Do you want her shot now or later?" This they said after a brief exchange of confusion. I always believed that a contract killer was a rabid dog who wouldn't let go of your leg even if you blew his brains off...I was wrong. This sudden shift in their loyalties was interesting.

"Would you wait till the morning?" I added a request.

"What do you mean by morning?" they talked like twins. "You think we have all the time...to kill?"

"Mind doing it when I go for my walk at seven?"

"Can you put the money down there?"

"Will you make it quick?" Whatever little love for Emarti I had left was talking now, though her whimpering behind me still brought on the sneeze.

"Why do you care so much, Uncle?" And they proceeded to tie-up Emarti to a shoe-rack in her room.

It now dawned on me that my smelliest problem was answered by answering questions with more questions. All my wedded life I had been looking for the right answers, whereas I should have just been asking myself the right questions. A ping-pong of words and emotions - my choice of sport.

I found Emarti lying facedown on her bed, and a tear snaked down my cheek and got lost in my beard. Now I had to find me a maid.

# *Chapter 5*

Things were going without a sneeze when I caught a bleeding cough. One of my rooms forgot to knock and worst of all, refused to answer my knock. That we were well past the business hours made it pretty unusual. I had employed a housekeeping agency to come in at eleven every night and leave the rooms, the beds and everything spanking by twelve. It was already ten-thirty as I pushed open the deaf and dumb door. At once, I knew the mess I was in.

There were two white naked corpses and a flushload of blood sprawled on the sheets. The woman lay face-down upon the man and his stony eyes stared at me over her bare shoulders. I remember her hiding her podginess behind him - which was natural - and peering over his shoulder, when they arrived. The bed looked like some loony artwork; looked like I had a night on my hands.

My first thought was to search for a letter. I saw it right away trying to hide under the guy's hand, and it said my guess was bang on. These two lovers wanted their people to suffer while they watched with quiet satisfaction from the dead. Innocently, little did they know how their greasy story was to be kept from everyone, except Emarti's ghost, because I too wanted my revenge for them dirtying my house without asking permission. And an interesting death is not always good publicity. I knew what to do.

First, I locked the room.

Housekeeping came and left.

I opened the room again and got working. The blood-stained everything, including their underclothes, were tied together in a tight ball and put away for an appropriate date. In stupid moments such as these, I had learned the virtue of silent endeavour. When a blind man is dying, no points for crying because a blind eye can't see you cry.

The next week was declared a holiday for me.

Then I went and got sixteen young vultures in a chicken van and left them in the room with their food. I was to come after four days and take them back to the slaughterhouse just outside town. In the charity business you can't afford to not be detached, so I took a train to the tea gardens in the hills. Nice weather.

I remember coming to the mountains with my stepmother. My father - who loved whores and beating Mother - had married a twenty-something widow and died of loose motions in his grocery shop down the road, all within a year of my mother's own lung attack. I lived with Nina for twenty-five years till I was forty. Had she too not died, Emarti would have been someone else's nightmare.

She'd let me watch her bathe.

Then she'd watch me bathe her.

The air in the city choked her in the hotter months, sending us scurrying to Didoli where her first husband had a small crumbling house. Somehow, people never smiled in the town or maybe, as I figured out later, they didn't care about us. Nina was over-affectionate with me when someone was around. I smelt a kind of defiance. But like I said, I don't go too deep into stories where I'd expect to find a bastard hiding.

It was her idea to sell the shop. How else were we to survive, she said. I thought it was a very clever thing to do with both of us least inclined to peddle toothpaste. It was also her idea to let me work in the blind school from my nineteenth year for two reasons: I had not done too well in getting grades and I could comfortably walk home for lunch. As I sat on the rock by our gate in Didoli, I remembered her a lot. A couple of birds of prey flying far above brought a smile back to my face.

I took a walk through the more cluttered part of town to smell the mustiness of woollens. The locals know me and don't know me. Unconsciously, I was heading towards a spot of research in a lane for lovers called Lower Lane. There was a huge difference in the way the houses here operated and the way I had figured out on my own. They worked ten-to-ten in the night and I worked ten-to-ten in the day. I wasn't greedy to make more, just curious to see how things happened after dark. The last I wanted was to become a run-of-the-loom workaholic.

"Looking for someone, Brother?"

Brother? Not Uncle? I turned around and was face-to-face with a salesman in police uniform. He began adjusting my scarf as he spoke between his teeth, "You've come to the right place, if you have. Walk up to any of the blue doors, not the red or white, and it'll open by itself."

Before I said 'unhh' he was gone. I had my answer - I would only be open to lovers during the day. I just didn't agree with delegating the running of my business to the law. Do you let an overindulgent donkey help a blind man cross the road?

Anyway, I did walk through one of the blue doors. It looked faded and familiar.

The stench was a wet slap. I steadied myself and caught hold of the lout blinking both eyes at me. He swallowed his juice as I pushed him to the corner.

"You were staring at me," I said, "is this how you welcome a guest? Take me inside, I have good news." He hesitated. I climbed the ladder into a loft-like space in the ceiling. He began calling out to somebody called Kamru in a nasal whine.

Kamru met me at the top of the ladder, extending a hand. I pulled myself into the hole. He stood aside and surveyed me, unsure of who I was. I told him to sit down and relax, I wasn't the bribe-collector. He was angry, it seemed, and probably just five-feet-two, without any shoes or hair on his head. By my calculations he would be in the region of very early fifties, but his skin was a premature field of furrows on a potato farm. His years of decay had knocked out two front teeth and rotted the rest. I looked around for a place to spit.

"Where can I spit?" I asked him to break the silence.

"Swallow it," he lisped.

"You enjoy living in a pigsty?"

"Yes."

I got up to go, "Nice talking to you." I dropped a clutch of money, as was the custom for any visitor to a house of pleasure, and went for the ladder.

"Why are you here? Do I know you?" he blabbered.

"Just came to confuse you," I replied.

"Tell me."

"Would you believe me if I said," I looked him straight in the eye, "I was Nina's stepson."

The effect was like very lazy poison. His eyes dilated gradually and his jaw stiffened. He broke into a lying smile, "Nina who?"

I walked out the way I came. A hungry beastly bird had lifted off my head and settled down on

Kamru's delicious hairless chest.

Taking a circuitous route, with a plate of stew and rice on the way, I reached home around twilight to find Kamru sitting on my rock by the gate.

"Nina's house is nice," he tried conversation.

"Nina who?" I returned his earlier sarcasm.

"Look, what do you want me to do?" The quiver in his voice suggested he had considered the implications of my visit and volunteered his cooperation to my undisclosed offer.

I wasn't making it easy for him. So I said, "I'll tell you when the time comes. I have three more days to murder here."

He went away, incomplete. I was sure his sleep had been snatched away.

I wondered if Nina and Emarti and those two bodies in the room and my father and my mother had anything in common. They were all dead. They died before their time. They died without giving a month's notice. They all had me.

But there was a story only one of them owned: Nina owned the brothel on Lower Lane. It was her husband's.

My father visited Didoli off and on, since my mother had been advised fresh air for her lung condition. Father had been told to avoid affection to avoid infection. He ended up spending a lot of time at Lower Lane and, naturally, met Nina. The rest even the blind can guess. The number of rooms in my father's house was probably inspired by these

vacations to the hills.

Soon, and uneventfully, it was time for me to go back.

The house seemed fine to me. My neighbours sneered beautifully in a choreographed manner. My eagerness was at the door before I managed to get out of the cab. How the birds had performed was my greatest excitement and I unlocked my anxiety with a vein throbbing in my neck. Had the experiment gone horribly wrong or terribly right? The house smelled not of death, but a decaying calm.

I flung open the room, and marvelled at the pungency in the air. Sixteen bald heads - I remembered Kamru - looked at me in deep contemplation. They were confused and somewhat unsure of whether to welcome me or act indifferent. I closed the door behind me and glided towards the spot where I had left the bodies. Filth and feathers blocked my path. The vultures made way rather reluctantly. It was now my turn to look blank.

Five bodies! Five bodies, neatly stripped to the bone, lay where I had left two. Upon the bed lounged two large skeletons and three lesser ones. I did a quick headcount: fourteen vultures; which meant two of the smaller skeletons were dead birds. And the third was obvious.

The dead girl had been carrying the dead man's child.

# Chapter 6

I sleep sitting up, it keeps my breathing clear. It also keeps my head uncluttered, otherwise too much blood rushes to my brain and makes me see comic dreams or hallucinations of which I can make no head or tail. But every so often I slide off the pile of pillows and find myself woken up by my dead father asking me how things are.

He has nothing new to say and beyond a point I don't find it funny anymore. It's the same old stuck record of a stupid song you no longer get pleased by.

*He sits against the wall of the bathroom, where I can see him.* I always leave the door half-open to make my room appear bigger. Before my mother died, I had a hairy dog without a name, which would sit at that very spot and keep looking at me. I was asked to get rid of him when he started biting random people near the house. I left him at all sorts of places I had never been to and he would come back, sometimes five days later. Father thought I was just fooling around and felt inclined to discipline me publicly with sarcasm. So I put the dog in layers of Father's coats, carried the bundle to the sea and buried him alive in twenty feet of saltwater.

Somehow Father always started our midnight talk with the dead dog as if he missed his jackets so much. *"You loved the dog, didn't you?" he would say.*

*"Stop it, Father, find yourself some new problem."* I am now sixty and he was around forty when he died, so it seems crazy listening to me calling him my father and all that. Ten years ago too I was ten years older than him. That's why I am not too amused by this deranged arrangement anymore, I'd rather sleep sitting up than fill my mind with his nonsense.

*"Should I tell you something?" he continues.*

*"I know," I cut him off, "your loose motions were rather sudden. You had porridge in the morning and that doesn't cause death by anal bleeding."*

*"Yeah. I think your stepmother was too kind to me that day."*

*"Don't call her my stepmother," I say, "it sounds evil. She has a name, you know."*

*"She had a name. Past tense. You called her Nina, I'm told. Did she say what she put in my breakfast?"*

*"You and your lousy conjectures, Father. You and your lousy conjectures. Why would she poison you? You brought her respect. Anyway, I don't feel like talking*

*to you, you've become a housewife. You've become my cruel crackpot mother."*

*"That brings me to your mother."*

*"Stop it."*

*He starts laughing. He roars so loud his head shakes with a severity. It begins rolling from side to side and back and forth and up and down. His hair grows longer and greyer. And he becomes my mother with a twitch in the left eye. I know this won't ever end.*

*"Hello, Son," she speaks softly.*

*"Ya. Go on."*

*"You eating well?"*

*"Don't try to be so nice, Mother, and come to the crux. Let me get over this and go back to sleep, if you are okay with your son waking up refreshed. I have started a business after all."*

*"I'm happy to hear that, Dear. But why did I have to suddenly die?"*

*"You died, you tell me." Another five minutes and I'll want to smother her with the pillows.*

*"There was one witness."*

*"Really?" I play along.*

*"You know who saw me thrash about and die?"*

*I knew, but I still said, "Father?"*

*"No."*

*"No?"*

*"No. A smelly grey pigeon."*

*"Oh!"*

*She gets a little restless, "And you know who killed me?"*

*"You had a lung attack, Mother. No one killed you."*

*Mother is screaming in a whisper, "I can't stand pigeons. My heart sinks, my hands shake. My head bursts with fear and my nose bleeds. You know pigeons make me go mad with panic. You know they suffocate me."*

*"Why didn't you run out, Mother? Why didn't you cry out?"*

*"You know why?" she pants, leaning against the bathroom door, "you know why?"*

*"Why, Mother?"*

*"Because the bloody doors were bolted from outside."*

*At this point I start to laugh and she hits the bathroom door with her fist.*

*"Someone left the pigeon in my room and locked the doors, Son."*

*I laugh madly now, this was the funniest part.*

*"And do you know who?"*

*"Who? Who? Who?" I jump on my bed and cry with exaggeration, "Who? Who? Who? Mother, was it Father?"*

*"It was you," she's all quiet at once. "Who tries and kills his own mother, Son? Why did you put the pigeon in my room?"*

*My eyes clasped tight in agony, I scream the truth, "Your coughing didn't let me sleep. Your cruelty didn't let me live. Your lunacy pushed me to the corner. Who tortures her own son, Mother, just because her man beats her? Strange way to show your motherliness. Now will you go away, I haven't too many minutes left to morning?"*

*"Was that it?" she looks up hopefully.*

*"No," I drive the last nail home, "Nina was better."*

# *Chapter 7*

Like a rifle bolt I get jolted back to the real world where a perfect kill had no ancestry. No brother-sister-cousin emotions. No motive whatsoever. My mother, father and Emarti were stupid deaths, though clever. The execution was perfect, but the suspicion could be imagined and believed.

I was back in business like clockwork. The Vulture Room had a large image of Emarti submerged in marigold mustiness and jasmine incense. I had to chase out all traces of the pungency that hit me when I first opened the room when you-know-when. I never used it for sex-commerce ever again. After the housekeeping boys disappeared every night, I would lock the house and drive around town in my father's grocery truck. This was also the time when trucks were permitted within city limits. It kept me from falling asleep and the past from taunting me. I had me for company, which was perfect.

Off and on I would slow down for a bunch of

drunks and drop them somewhere away from the law. They never thanked me and I never spoke, just slowed down. It was a silent ritual where some kind of kindness simply happened. They sat in the back of the rusty transport and I saw them in the mirror, half-asleep holding on to the sides as we lurched along. Only once did they disrespect and threaten to hurt me, but they were piss-drunk and I forgave their mothers for the fault of their milk. So often it was the same group, which felt a right over being carried back home by a magical vehicle appearing out of nowhere, each night. So often I parked at the gates of a late movie and sat or slept through the last half hour. The noise and the voices played on me like a broken song. So often I was gently woken up in an empty hall by the usher in a way that my own mother never did.

*Only Nina would reach out to me across the bed and say, "Open your eyes, you blindman's stick, you'll get left behind."* Emarti probably always hoped I'd never wake up. She looked good in the Vulture Room.

I remember sleeping through films in tongues I didn't understand. Very poor people watched these, I noticed, to manage turmoil and because they had no place to sleep. There were too many poor people too desperate to do anything for a night of dreams: getting sloshed was one way, getting to sleep with a stranger was the other. On my way back home, there never was a day when an urchin never stood in the path of my truck and asked for a lift to nowhere. I stopped for hopeless drunks, but these kids had mothers standing in the shadows egging them on.

One night, I found a ten-year-old boy dragging his feet along a dark road. He was muttering to himself and swung his small bundle at invisible demons. He heard the truck behind him and waved for me to stop. I went on for a while and then slowed down. He ran towards me. A slipper came off, he looked back a moment, and flung the other one off as well. Soon he was breathing heavily, looking up at my window. He had a gash between the chin and the lower lip. No one saw him get in.

He pulled himself into a bundle and looked straight ahead with bleary eyes as if he had already told me where he wanted to go. I gave him a cone of peanuts I had picked up at the cinema and watched him break the shells with his teeth and create a mess all over him. An alien warmth swept over me.

I was ten when Father made me sit on the counter-top of his shop after school. The customers would ruffle my hair and offer me things to eat that I'd refuse. This boy hadn't anyone to glare at him and make him say 'no thank you' like my father did. I envied his freedom. The cut below his lip had begun bleeding again very gently.

"Who hurt you?" I said.

He had dozed off. He turned his head towards me and looked blankly with a drooping jaw. His tongue slid out and he licked the snaking blood off. I shivered.

He opened his mind to speak and clamped up.

"Tell me," I coaxed, "did your father hit you?"

He shook his head.

"Mother?"

"No, I only have you."

I laughed, "But you hardly know me, Bastard."

"I only know you." He was staring directly at me. His big eyes were getting bigger.

I kept driving silently for some time, and even struck my knee to see if I was still asleep in the theatre. The boy kept looking at me. I was a bit unnerved now, so I came to the point as I do in situations beyond my capacity.

"Should I ask you to get off my truck and start walking in the dark again?" I caught him by his hair and shook him.

"You will never do that," he didn't resist, "you are now under my spell."

This time I laughed louder and a lot more nervously. He was throwing peanut shells all around the cabin. I had never seen anything like it. A boy, barely ten, was getting me bothered late at night. He was mocking me, quite unafraid of the dark and a bearded stranger. He went on tossing the peanut shells at the windshield.

"I said stop doing that," I shouted.

He did not stop. I raised my left hand and struck him across the face. He flew over the seat and hit the door. I saw the speed-needle climb. The boy lay there crumpled forever. And when I turned to glance at him, he was looking at me.

"You hit me," he said, "and, for no great reason."

I stopped the truck and kicked the freak out. There are people in this world who get pleasure out of pain, I know, but the bar for that had just been lowered. I saw the boy dust himself and walk down the road again, kicking stones. He was mad, I concluded, he should have been eliminated. Madness scares me. He reminded me of me. I reminded me of my mother. She always hit me for no real reason.

I had barely forgotten the incident, when I stopped one night for a woman in her forties. There were these days when I took me for a night-ride out of town. I would drive away for four hours, then stop for tea at a sleepy thatched hut and drive back in time for work.

The tin crate was rolling away noisily in the darkness without a doubt and, in a blink, a ghost of a woman drifted into the headlights. I don't know what made me stop. She could have been a trap. She pulled herself up the half-ladder.

"My son has come under a car," she cried, "I must reach town early morning."

I said nothing, just started the engine. She was dabbing her eyes and clutching a plastic bag she had hurriedly collected. A very tragic woman, I gathered. Her clothes reeked of sweat that comes from working in the sun in the fields. It is different from a city worker's or a sex worker's smell. More spicy. She wore two musty pigeon feathers untidily in her bun and one dangled close to her neck.

"I have no one but him," she was telling a stranger her weakness, "and we have no money. All he earns he spends. Sends me whatever little he can." I wasn't even listening.

It was almost three in the morning. There was not a beast on the road. The woman kept chattering away in her grief. I stopped the truck. The woman wondered why, but didn't seem scared. I looked at her, she smiled. I brought my hands to her neck and strangled her struggling form till it was still. Madness scares me. I sat quietly for a few minutes. A great big surge of pleasure seemed to pass through me. The smell of the crushed feather became stronger. I pushed the body out, with my feet, after an hour. There was no motive. Perfect.

# *Chapter 8*

Nina always said that making love to someone and killing someone were one and the same. At our house in Didoli we spent a lot of time doing little much. She went out in the morning sometimes, and came back by lunch. She wasn't much of a cook and still I was happy she pottered around in the kitchen to come up with mishmash unfit for the weak-hearted. She chortled seeing my wrinkled nose. She laughed even louder at my ignorance.

"Why did I kill the dog, Nina?" I asked her.

And she made me sit down at her feet. She said, "Did you like it?"

"The dog or the killing?"

"Killing the dog, Stupid."

"Yeah, I guess," I was sure.

She put oil in my hair and went on, "Do you like oil in your hair?"

"Hmmm."

"Then what guilt is there in pleasure? Violence is normal, Son. Aren't we born violently? Violence is pleasurable. Pleasure is normal." She called me 'son' only when she felt responsible. "Killing someone is like making love." She would then bathe me and kill me with love to stop my questions. I was only five years younger than her and such a fool.

"Where does our money come from?" I wanted to know.

"You remember your dad's shop?" she asked pointing to her peeping belly-button, "It's in here. Finished. So what do we eat? Nice question."

That day she took me to Lower Lane and left me for the day. In the evening, she walked me away from her brothel and asked me if I liked the answer. I said I had another question first.

"Now what?" she laughed.

"Why did you let Father die?"

"There was no pleasure in a grocery store. He was already dead when I met him."

Nina's answers were so firm, I nodded. Of course, it's better to die forever than whenever.

"Your father killed your mother for me." I didn't correct her and keeping the truth from her made me feel guilty. She was looking at me like a heron deep in thought. She said, "I'll tell you something even bigger, though not today."

The day came. It was raining firecrackers. Nina and I were watching the whiteness shroud the hills. We had gone out in the rain to open a couple of blocked drains and had stayed out for an hour sitting on the rock by the gate.

A dark form, followed closely by a small shadow, approached the house. It was going to the back door when Nina called out, "I'm here, Sattu."

Sattu walked with a limp. He carried a large packet in his arms and a boy of four held on to his shirt-tail. I saw only a bit of his snotty face. The man looked at me. Nina said, "It's alright, he's my son. And what's that you're hiding behind you?"

"He's Kamru, my son. He'll be your man when I'm gone. Starting him off early in the business."

"Get down to it then," she spoke not without a sudden annoyance, so typical of her.

"Shouldn't we go inside?" he said, covering the packet. She didn't answer, which normally meant 'no'. Sattu pulled a yellow plastic sheet over all of us and gently opened his load. I could feel his bitter tobacco breath too close to Nina's head. He felt like an encroachment.

A baby cried.

He was holding a newborn and she was examining it as a doctor. She checked if it was a boy or a girl, it was a girl. Finally, she asked him to cover it up nicely and declared, "It's okay. Could have been fairer." Sattu began to protest and she waved him away. Kamru looked over his shoulder, once outside the gate, and hurried on behind the baby's plaintive bleat. We sat for another hour watching the rain without a word.

"There are people in this world," she told me when we were inside, "who feed thousands of people." I waited as she wove her logic. "There are also people who are merely food. They have no other purpose." My expression made her smile; she punched me on the arm.

"Love is what makes the world turn. Why does a parent take all the trouble to teach a son? To sit with homework? Why does anyone take any trouble in this world? It's all love." That sounded pretty simple to me. "Why do the poor not take trouble with their children?"

"There is no love in poverty," she continued. "Poor people don't love. They fool you into believing they do, but they don't. They shed saltless tears when someone dies. Like a bitch, a poor mother forgets her loss within two days. For her love is a convenience to get food." I had seen it on Lower Lane, but what had all this to do with the baby I saw?

"There is a world you will not see. Most people don't. Some people just won't. It is the world of the people who feed the thousands. That baby you saw," she had a hand on my shoulder, "was a newborn."

I could see she was having strong doubts about moving forward with the story, so I said, "It's fine, Nina, you can tell me. I think it is time."

"What you saw on Lower Lane was people feeding the people who feed many more. Your father came there too, to be fed. He gave me this in return." She took off her earring. She took my hand in her hand and in one quick jab pierced my fingertip with the pin on it. I watched her suck the bleeding.

"Our pain is our pleasure," she was saying. "Pain is always a pleasure."

"And the newborn baby?" I prompted.

"Sacrifice," she said quietly.

"Sacrifice, Nina?"

"When a new factory comes up, it comes with a furnace. The furnace needs to be fed. A baby must be sacrificed. Thrown to the flames to keep the fires burning forever to feed the thousands. Where do you think babies come from?"

"The poor," I ventured.

"Yeah. Where there is no love."

"So that baby goes into the furnace," I put my head on Nina's shoulder, "to start a factory?"

"We are in the business of creating love where there is none. Creating pain for pleasure. You asked me where our money comes from."

I had the answer. Whether the baby girl was sacrificed to start a factory or sustain our brothel was irrelevant - she was born to feed us.

Years later, Nina slit her wrists.

As I bent close to her drained face, she whispered, "This is beautiful, Son, painful and beautiful."

"Why, Nina?" She had been chatty that morning. I saw no need for this.

"I wanted to experience the greatest pleasure," she winked at me and called out to the nurse, a decent-looking one in torn stockings. "Are you married, Sister?" she asked.

"No, Ma'am," said the surprised girl.

"Why don't you marry my son?" Nina was desperate to go, "He may be a little older, but he's rich. And he's alone. I won't survive the night. Will you?"

The nurse just looked at her, writhing in her mind. It was love taking pains, I knew. I don't know what came over the young girl in starched whites, she nodded a promise to the woman staring at her. Maybe her pain back home was a monster far greater. Funnily, I wasn't a part of the transaction being made on my behalf.

"What's your name?" Nina spoke her last words.

"Emarti," said the girl.

Nina's funeral was lonely. Her heartbeats were replaced by Sattu's gloomy drumbeats. I was angry with Nina for dying. I was angry at my parting gift for the very same reason: she marked the saddest moment of my existence. She replaced everything I loved with nothing I cared about. My heart had been yanked out and the hollow stuffed with torn stockings. It was insanely unfair. Father and

Mother made their first appearances, grinning at me. I cried within and sneezed without as Nina's smell was smothered by Emarti's pineapple flavour. My marriage was a funeral.

# *Chapter 9*

I must have been forty at Nina's funeral. The first time I went back to Didoli alone was ten years after that, lest some old memory pounded me. The house was a skull found in the bushes. The brothel was running on its own by Sattu or whomever, I didn't care. I liked living in anything but yesterday. I did touch the house, sit on the rock by the gate and return refreshed many a times, but it took me ten more years to confront the new improved Kamru in Nina's den.

My own visitors had grown in quality. Smelly flesh had been overcome by odours hastily splashed or sprayed. Only I knew who came and went and even I didn't ask who was who. By their swagger I could tell what profession they pimped. The college kids and mechanics' sons had been ousted by accountants and teachers and traders and a steep rise in my room rent. One of my quietest guests was a wrinkled magistrate who would take the day off without telling anyone at home, I presumed. I never worked night-shift, as I had promised myself. I had even started buying stuff for the house. Investing in infrastructure, as they say.

I was out shopping one Sunday. That's right, I had begun giving myself a day off every fortnight. It was a huge store of lights where I stood gawking at a chandelier the size of God's earring. If it fell, a dozen modern aristocrats would be crushed to a mangled bony chandelier themselves. I heard voices.

"You are trying your luck," a man was saying good-naturedly. A woman laughed. I had heard the laugh before.

The woman said, "I'm trying you. Is it too much? I thought it could look good in the guest balcony. No?"

"Yah, whatever," the man wasn't really bothered, "take it if you must. I'll imagine it came with the bride."

I turned around and came face to face with his bride. I had seen the face before. She too recognized me for a brief moment, I believe, and then looked right through me. I had most definitely seen her somewhere very prominently.

"Should we go home?" her voice, down to a loud whisper, faltered now, "I feel a cramp coming on." She was holding her husband's arm and leading him to the door.

"Can you wait up a bit," he brushed her off. The suddenness of her mood had unhinged him.

She stood outside the shop tapping her foot, while he took time paying for an indecent-looking lamp. The kind you talk about when people come home visiting.

"Your wife is annoyed," I interfered, "you better hurry."

"Never hurry a surgery," he said out of context. He seemed like the sort who'd think up smart things to say and then look for occasions to say them to be considered smart.

"You are a doctor?"

"Nah, a butcher of men," he laughed, again for effect.

"I think your wife doesn't like my talking to you. She's angry or something."

He extended a delicate hand, "Then I must be off. And, by the way, I think you should show someone the lump on your neck. It may be nothing actually." He backed out of the glass door with an unnecessary smile.

My hand went to my nape.

I had no one to take me to the butcher.

My lump felt lonely.

Six months later, I had not shown the protrusion to anyone. I had forgotten completely. Had Nina been around, she would have swept me to the surgeon and made a ceremony of it. What reminded me of it, however, was almost nothing in the glossy section of the Friday newspaper.

It was a picture of the doctor saying 'cheese' at a social. He was red-faced and hanging on to his equally happy wife in green silk. I smiled, but the boy in the background blew my mind to shrapnel. He was serving drinks in a dark uniform and a white cap to distinguish his type from the more distinguished. He wasn't looking into camera, he was staring at the silk wife. Of course I know him, I laughed at my forgetfulness. I knew also, at once, who the doctor's bride was. Now if the doctor was found dead, I'd know what happened. Photographs, no matter how posed, are a true picture of human conflict frozen in a second.

Green silk was the girl who released me from my zipper, and the rough uniform was the boy she spent an hour with in my house. How could I misplace them? The smelly lovers that gave me the idea for the house were the new wife and the old waiter. I wanted to tell the doctor he too had a lump, I just didn't have the heart.

One thing struck me about my profession: it was totally professional. The enthusiastic girl from my zipper circumcision had chosen to coldly look through me by the time I needed a tumour surgery. I was fast eroding whatever little emotions I had saved up.

I still did not take an appointment with the clinic. I invited a somewhat distant relation of Nina's to take care of me instead. The house was getting too big for my boots.

# *Chapter 10*

Kamru came to stay.

The brothel on Lower Lane was technically mine and I could do what I wanted with it, so I sold it. The house remained intact for a purpose other than serving Nina's memory. I would, however, know the real reason for retaining it only much later. My own mind was starting to keep certain secrets from me or possibly, like a circus bear, my actions were beginning to precede my thoughts. I wasn't so sure of Kamru's dropping in, nor of him occupying Emarti's room as if it was his own, until the deed was done. I realised I had unconsciously invited him in for two reasons: one, because I had taken away his livelihood and two, I could never be cruel to the more pleasant memories of Nina. In fact, anything reminding me of Nina caressed my solitude more so now than ever. Somehow, I felt this kept fragments of her alive.

Kamru was a bat who had difficulty sleeping in the night and I had promised to never work after dark. When he insisted he was right in harvesting the night, I started taking him with me on my drives merely to keep an eye on him. While I slept sitting up, he took the truck wherever he wanted to. My father and mother too stopped bothering me. And he became the dog I had drowned.

It was Kamru who took me for my neck check. The doctor thought he had come to correct his hyena-like posture and told him to lie down on his belly. We realized the mistake only when the name of the patient was read out by the burping, cursing nurse. I felt a fear rise inside me as she touched my shoulder to roll down my shirt collar. Not because I was afraid to discover death sitting there, but for my undiluted phobia for sisters of all makes. They remind me of Nina dripping blood, the unfairness of it and, worst of all, a suffocation called Emarti.

She screamed.

My right hand had grabbed her hair and thrown her against the wall. Kamru leapt between us and I knew he was on her side. The doctor was yelling for security. I sat down quietly and looked at my hand. A clump of grey hair made me want to vomit blood. The nurse was trying to scare me with dangerous eyes filled red with fake tears.

"Cool down," the doctor told her.

"He tried to kill me," the woman was pretending to be really hurt. She began wailing when the guards rushed in. Kamru came between them and me. He was on my side now. What a strange dog.

They refused to see my neck after that, saying I needed another appointment since that woman's dance had eaten into my time and a hundred other patients were out there awaiting death. Kamru pushed the doctor to a corner and, with his tobacco-blackened tongue, licked his right cheek twice from the chin to the ear. We went away amidst a lot of noisy laughter that belonged to us.

We forgot the lousy lump like serious news.

"Let me show you something," Kamru said to me the other night in the truck. He probably imagined I was low after the hospital disrespected us and wanted to distract me. I smiled my consent only to humour him, though I did not feel the need to be mothered.

The truck took a quick U-turn and then veered off on to a dusty lane crammed with houses already asleep. Soon, we had left the city behind and an awkward moon was lighting up the paddy fields. Everything looked black and silver. I glanced at Kamru humming a song only he knew. He stopped the truck.

"We must walk from here," he said.

"The bloody thing is blocking the road," I asked, "is that okay?"

"No one comes here after dark."

I followed the dog on a thin strip of earth

between two paddy fields. There was a yellow light a half-mile away, and it was pulling us to it. My shoes were squishy in mud and Kamru had the sense to walk barefoot. As we neared, a voice became clearer, not the words. A faint glow from a lamp lit up what appeared to be a mass of bricks under a large tree. I had no idea Kamru was so saintly.

"It's our temple," he whispered.

"Ours?" I whispered back.

"Our community."

I have no community to speak of, but all I said was, "Oh." He seemed pleased at my response and quickened his pace. The last time I visited a place of worship was the Vulture Room in my house with a garlanded Emarti. All guests had made it a habit to touch her picture before entering or being entered. I had created a goddess out of a bitch. A goddess out of a doggess.

"Put a cloth over your head," Kamru was saying. I saw before me a granite slab with a slit running down the centre. Below the dark-stained stone sat a large earthen pot and a strange sour smell emanated from it. Kamru kneeled down and brought his head lower to touch the slab.

A woman's voice came from somewhere in the darkness around. "Why is your friend not bending? Is he not afraid?"

Kamru saw the look in my eye and replied, "Can't bend his knees."

But I don't easily lie, so I said, "Show yourself. I can't talk to the night." I sat down a little distance off. Kamru looked a bit uncertain, with his mouth open. There was a long pause in which I thought I heard low whispers. At last, I felt a hand on my shoulder. It travelled up to my neck and touched the mass of hardened flesh.

"Is this it?" a woman's voice again.

"Yes," said Kamru.

"Does it pain?"

"When I press it," I replied. The hands squeezed the lump and I ground my teeth. How could she have known about it? I wondered.

"Is it spicy or bitter or salty or sour?" the voice asked.

"What? The pain? How would I know?" I laughed.

"Is it sharp or dull?"

"Sharp. Like an acid being poured in the ear."

"How would you know?" she was playing my game with me.

"Why don't you try putting acid in your ear?" The ambient silence grew louder. No word was spoken for an hour. I was sleepy and, I think, I must have dozed off sitting against a stone wall. Kamru remained on his knees all the while. A thin bleat woke me up.

A young lamb was lying on the slab and Kamru's fierce hands held its neck down. The animal's struggle stopped suddenly and I noticed a river of blood pour itself into the pot below. How long this was going on, I don't know. The sight had poetry. Kamru carried the pot towards me.

"Take your shirt off," the voice had not gone away. I did as I was told. Kamru smeared my torso with the goat's warm blood, I felt like the mud in my shoes. "Drink this," I was told and a small cup appeared over my shoulder.

It was some sweet milky stuff.

I woke up in the truck. Kamru was driving bleary-eyed. He turned his head and smiled hazily.

"What happened?" I asked.

"Nothing much," he said.

There was no trace of blood on me. "How did I reach the truck? Where's the blood?"

Kamru spoke through his grin, "I carried you."

"Where's the blood?"

He started humming his song. We were going at a gentle pace, five miles from sunrise. My head was still spinning. I grabbed Kamru's arm. The truck swerved a bit. "Where's the blood?" I asked for the third time, "Did you bathe me too?"

"Sort of," he tried to evade a direct answer and I wanted the reason. "Did you notice?"

"What?" I was annoyed.

"The lump on your neck."

My hand went to my neck. There was nothing there, except a very thorny pain. I closed my eyes.

Kamru gave me a small bottle to drink from. I took a quick swig of the same white poison and passed out.

"What do doctors know," I heard Kamru mumble in my sleep.

It was many months later that he told me how my blood was washed off. "Six pups and a bitch licked you clean," he said in a drunken state one night. "The mass on the neck was bitten off by the keeper of the temple. She slept with you."

# *Chapter 11*

I was glad Kamru had taken over the running of the rooms. He had been a manager all his life, after all. He learnt the value of day time customers, and that they had the ability to pay many times more and came with their own women. You simply sat back and managed traffic so there were no collisions. Like I said, the quality of the guests was going up considerably from the very affluent to the very powerful. Every couple needs a room for a couple of hours, nothing more nothing less.

I was already thinking expansion. Kamru said we must first diversify to the night slot with new products. I wanted to start a whole chain of houses in all big towns. Kamru said we would lose control over the franchises if we didn't use force. I told him to shut up and not try and tell me how to run my business. He stopped coming for the truck rides to show he was sulking. Having sacrificed so many babies, he was behaving like one.

I didn't quite like the idea of leaving him alone at home at night because I had found something under his bed, which made me believe he was secretly working on a new project. Kamru's ambition was disturbing for me.

It so happened, I had a rather influential gentleman with a lady in one of the rooms and this person knocked within minutes. I found that odd, and opened the door with a worried scratching of my beard.

"Anything the matter?" I asked.

"The lady likes to read during the act," he said, "and she has forgotten her book."

"How can I help?"

"Get her a book, of course," he replied with some firmness.

"How about a newspaper?" I suggested.

"I said book." Now he was deeply annoyed. I sent Kamru off to look for a book, any book, though I wasn't sure he knew what that actually was. The guest knocked on the door every few minutes and demanded to see the material at once. I wasn't anxious or anything, but I did troop down to Kamru's room to see if Emarti had left any of her pulp behind. It was a tricky situation, I knew, with barely ten minutes to finish my search because experience told me that one of the rooms would surely begin knocking soon.

The door opened with a push. A wave of nausea

hit me. This is where I had spent twenty years of my life with an unending sneeze. And as if the memory was enough, I started sneezing madly. She had left behind the pineapple flavoured air to kill me. I held my breath and searched somewhere between Kamru's return and the next knock on a door.

Kamru had an odour only he possessed. He brought it from Lower Lane and at times I had to hold my breath because it seemed he was the chamber gassing me. There was an untidiness Emarti would not approve of. Her nurse mentality liked the interiors starched and ironed to a state of sterilization. I preferred Kamru's filth to her emasculating perfection. My eyes searched for a book, but my mind was looking for an answer to a vague hunch that my dog was not as faithful as I'd want him to be. He wagged his tail a little too vigorously when I came back in the night.

I went through the pockets of his tough watchman's coat. Nothing, just a piece of wire and some damp tobacco. In an inner pocket in the lining was a wrinkled picture of a woman, accidently crumpled in the wash. I had put it back in when I decided to take another look as the face had a familiar frown. It was Nina.

I sat down. This was Nina's house too, and there she was living in a smelly hole in a dirty coat. My head spun asking for air. I almost rushed out of the door and then stopped. My search was not yet complete. A gnawing rat in my head told me to go down on all fours and feel under the bed. I did. My hand hit a solid box of rusty roughness and as I pulled it half out from under the dark and dust. I heard the main door open. I grabbed a small thing lying on the lid and pushed the box back with my foot. Kamru was standing at the door.

"Someone is knocking," he informed me.

"I came to see if Emarti had a book lying around," I said walking past him. "Did you find anything?"

"Did you?" he asked too casually.

"I have no time for games. Where's it?" He held out a thin text book on 'mango cultivation in the kitchen garden' and I scratched my head thinking of how to present it to the lady. I could barely imagine the happy effect the contents would have on her performance.

Half way up the stairs with the manual, I opened my other hand to see what I'd snatched from the top of Kamru's box. Sitting on Nina's washed out picture was Kamru's tiny rubbery rat-eaten secret - a baby's big finger or a girl's little one. I stared, trying to make some sense. But Kamru had his distinct ways of solving problems of his own and of his many worlds' - probably passed down from his nicotine-soaked father. I thought of the little boy hanging on to Sattu's shirt-tail back in Didoli some forty years ago.

# *Chapter 12*

I didn't bring the finger up for enquiry. And Nina's picture went and lived in my pocket. I decided to start a new service for the night simply to not leave Kamru alone at home. If something had to fill the night slot, it would not be anyone's idea but mine.

I had an insight. A little research turned it into a concept. I had tasted success and here was its sister-in-law sitting unclothed at my door. My right hand almost patted my shoulder at the inventiveness. Kamru sulked harder for the very same reason, I reckoned.

One of the guests left behind a slim clutch under the mattress. She would have imagined it was the safest place, right under her, and when she didn't come back for it, I knew she had forgotten where she lost it. I found her card inside and called her. She took a century to recollect who I was and then promised to call me back, which she did within the hour.

"Sir, you had called about my bag," she spoke in a secretive manner not without urgency.

"I thought you had a problem remembering who I was," I said, "I'm glad you've regained your powers."

She was silent for a while and then said as if she was hiding a bastard, "I'm a thousand miles away in another city where I live. I come to yours every weekend."

"You are a businessperson like me?" I added.

She did not like that, and very angrily informed me she was a student.

"What's a student doing in my house?" I asked in such innocence to lay to rest my doubt. "What is she doing a thousand miles away from home?"

This time the silence was infinite. I had an entire night to kill. I was also enjoying this. While I waited for an answer, I tried to figure out what she looked like. Was she the one with the single silver streak or the girl with the cough or the one who kept brushing off the man's hand each time he tried to put it around a little below her waist?

At last she spoke, "Is it important to know why I was there?"

"Absolutely," I replied, "I know everything about you except everything."

She laughed and relaxed a bit. "Can I trust you to keep a story, Uncle?" I said nothing. "Anyway," she cleared her throat like the girl with the cough, "what is there to hide for someone who has nothing more to lose?" She was trying to bring tears to my eyes and I had none. So I asked her if she was a prostitute.

"On the weekends," she answered as if she had just discovered a truth about herself, "I guess I am. Does that shock you, Uncle?"

"No," I tried to put it mildly for her sake, "I don't easily die. But tell me, why waste money on travel when you need it so much? You do it for money, no?"

"No," she was suddenly calm.

"I'm listening."

"I like it. Money is an extra. I love to sleep with people I hardly know, it's a game I like to play."

"Since when?" I liked the freshness of the idea.

"Two years. Second year of college. This man I knew disappeared," she was beginning a long tale of self-pity, so I cut her off.

"Why come to this city, aren't there men in yours?"

"The grass is juicier on the other side. Familiarity is a bitch on this side. I started it all when I wanted a new bag."

I wasn't interested in the inspiration for her reluctant entrepreneurship, I was probing for the sustainability of a germ in my head. If a girl must come to the city to earn quick money or fast emotions, then she must have a place for a couple of hours.

"Where do you stay when you come?" I asked.

"Where else?" she made my question sound silly.

"How many of you come here to study?"

"You'll be shocked."

"Sounds good," I laughed. She too laughed and went into a wheezing fit. I cut the call.

Two days later she was on the phone again.

"When can I collect my stuff?" she asked after lying how her neighbour had died in the last two days and she couldn't sleep.

"Whenever," I told her, "whenever you bring two more. I'll put you up free for the night."

"Free?"

"Yeah."

"What's the idea, Uncle?"

"I don't do it for money, Kid. I just love what I do."

Her 'okay' didn't sound so okay to me because somewhere at the back of my brain was a lout of a doubt called Kamru. I had noticed him hanging outside the room, I strongly presume, she was in that night. There was something going on not in tune with my song. Neither the whore nor the mangy cur had the eyes to see what was waiting behind the curve of her pomposity.

# Chapter 13

The weekend arrived late Friday night. The bell rang pretending to be unsure of the address. The girl with the cough stood on the front steps. She stepped in like a fresh bride all shy and important. I asked her where the others were.

"I'm the sacrificial goat, the bait," she said walking in. I thought of the one at the altar and then wondered why an altar is called an altar - a place where a couple of people go to die for life. I was a goat too, and I had created my own altar in my house.

The girl was saying, "Aren't you going to come inside?" and for some reason known only to her, started giggling. I led her up the stairs, past the Vulture Room and to a cave next to mine. She was not very happy or at least her silence was not.

"Don't like it?" I asked directly.

"I like windows," she sat down on the bed. "I like to look out when I'm with someone."

"This room is free," I explained to her, "freedom

is something else. Do not disrespect my welcome."

"Come, you forced me to come, Uncle. You kidnapped my clutch and I'm here as ransom. So let's not play this game okay? I want a better room."

"Why did you leave your bag behind?" I wanted to tell her I wasn't born the day before. "There was nothing in it to force a girl's return. Now what was it you were thinking? I could take a blade and slice open the truth. Tell me."

She watched her fingers play with each other.

"I saw you talk to my slave," I continued, "I saw you look at him. You know him, don't you?" She kept squeezing the neck of her right thumb. "I know how many college girls come here on the weekends to make money, but you are not one of them. What do you study?"

"Nothing. I'm a bad student."

"No you are not," I couldn't help smiling, "you are not a bad student. You are not a student at all. You are a bad whore."

She got up suddenly and went for her bag. I caught her by the arm and pushed her back on the bed.

"You are one of Kamru's girls. I won't ask you why you're here, I'll just tell you where you must go. And a word of this to the dog and you'll taste my blade. Are you Kamru's girl?"

She looked out of the non-existent window.

"Are you?"

She nodded, biting her lip uncertainly.

"I have a house in Didoli," I put my hand on her head and gently grabbed her hair, "you must take care of that."

"Please don't hurt me," she whimpered. I loosened my grip a bit.

"You will stay there and wait for my instructions." She nodded. "Now get out of here."

"Where will I go at this hour?"

"What have you to lose?" I reminded her.

"Please let me stay the night."

"Without windows?"

She didn't answer and I like answers.

"Without windows?"

"Yes."

"A word of this to the dog," I didn't know how to carry the threat from there, and she helped out.

"You'll serve me blades for dinner."

I like people who are spontaneously honest, so I returned the favour. "You are out of work because I sold the business," I said, "now it is my duty to see you fed."

"Blades?"

I slapped her cheek lightly and told her to go sleep on an empty stomach for deceiving me for so long. I locked the door. She was on the train before dawn, in a steel room with too many windows.

# *Chapter 14*

Her name was Bidiya. I gave her an allowance and clear instructions to keep Nina's house clean in every sense. No visitors whatsoever. From there in the hills she was to manage the traffic of the kind of college girls she had pretended to be. She was the booking office for the night shift at my house four hundred miles away. Undergraduates from four distant cities could now pay for their education, and their new handbags, without risking their lives in an uncertain land of greener grass. The basic philosophy remained the same: you bring your own partner and pay the rent by the hour. Interestingly, girls from the city liked the day, while the tourists loved the night. Kamru was both happy and dazed.

Driven by pleasure of the business I had become what I had sworn never to be: a workaholic. Kamru too had no free time, and I found no new fingers when I popped into his room on the days he ran errands. He had no idea where his whore had disappeared. He did open his mouth a bit to ask me and then left it half-open, unsure of what I may accuse him of. Otherwise, we were booze-brothers.

It was during one of the nights that something shifted in my loneliness.

I was waiting in my room for a bell to ring to open a door. I had long ago replaced knocking with ringing of the bell as in hotels. Room 4 trilled. I had caught a whiff of the short-haired history student's moist armpit on the landing and I must admit, it lingered in my head for a minute too long. I jumped up to release her. I wanted to see her face. I hoped she was with a decent man. I wondered where she came from. I rushed down two steps at a time and found Kamru inserting his key.

"Get me a blanket," I barked at him. He took his time with the key. "I'll do that. Get me a blanket." He looked surprised this time. Something in his eyes told me to calm down and not give him the pleasure of my anxiety. He too wanted to know what I was suddenly so keen about. He stood aside and let me thrust my key in the lock.

"Why, have you gone deaf? Can you get me a blanket?" I was literally pushing him down the stairs for the rarest of rare requests. A blanket was needed in these parts only to hurriedly bury a body, and he saw no reason then. I could hear the bell ring furiously in my room. Kamru slunk away.

My shaking hands unlocked the door. My brain was beating in its room unsure of everything. There was a taste of burnt tobacco on my tongue and a cold breath ran down my back like an uncertain emotion. A man's voice on the other side was telling me to hurry up and get him out of the woman, in a far cruder language.

The door swung open. The man strode out. He flung a fistful of money at the girl and glared at me as if I had made the mistake of fathering him. I never saw him again.

The girl cast a glance at her reflection in the mirror leaning against the wall and lifted her arms to push a long wooden hairpin into a tiny bun. The smell of her underarms danced around me. After nearly twenty years, I had my first arousal.

Kamru was watching me watch her.

The girl was around twenty. She had a very broad lower jaw protruding out and sunken eyes like lumps of dismay. Her hair was coarse and thinning with premature greys here and there. She wore a mismatched maroon lip liner above the curve of her very dark lips and, much to my surprise, a cheap business suit of smooth green shiny material.

"How much, Uncle?" she asked in a hoarse voice.

I told her.

She handed me the charge for three hours and then changed her mind.

"What if I stayed the night?" she said.

"Same cost," Kamru butted-in and turned to

me, "here's your blanket, Boss."

"Put it in the room," I told him, "the lady is staying the night."

The girl protested, "No, I was only asking."

"She is staying," I said, "it is late."

"But I must go eat."

"She's eating with us," I informed Kamru without asking anyone's permission. He glanced at me, his eyes filled with questions. "What! First time you've seen me?" I snapped.

"Seems."

I let the comment pass. "What's your name?"

"Nothing," the girl replied quietly.

I just shrugged a shoulder accepting her anonymity. The fragrance of her sweat had crawled all over the staircase. I walked back to my room.

"Are we having her for dinner, Boss?"

I turned to glare at Kamru. The girl was looking at both of us as she would a game of street tennis.

"Get her something to wear for the night."

"Emarti's?"

"No," I shouted, "get her some decent clothes."

"Why does she need decent clothes?" Kamru mocked. I felt my head throb a drumbeat.

I closed my door behind me. I sat down on the bed and sobbed.

## *Chapter 15*

Dinner was different.

We, the three of us, sat silently casting uncoordinated glances at each other. I was feeling melancholic for some unknown reason. I hadn't cried in recent years and my salmon-pink whites of the eyes choked Kamru over every morsel he partook. The clatter of the cutlery was putting my teeth on edge, and I had to destroy the monotony.

"What's your name?" I asked the girl the second time.

"Nothing," she was quick.

"Well, Nothing, do you come here often?"

"Once a month, maybe. Why, you never saw me before? My third time."

"Same guy?"

"Of course not. Whoever does that?"

"Tell me," I stopped eating, "do I know you from the past? Say, when I was younger. Have we met before?"

"Were you young twenty years ago?" she

laughed and choked, tears in her eyes. "That's when I was born," she said, gulping a glass of water.

Kamru simply listened-in. He was more curious than the neighbourhood witches who stuck at their windows watching the house. He had, I noticed, stopped eating since the dialogue began.

"You don't seem hungry," I told him. He was so deep in thought, I thought he was only pretending to look thoughtful. I had to pour chicken broth over his sleepy hand.

"What Boss, you are acting strange tonight," he sounded hurt.

"You are the one not eating. And now you want to sulk." Somehow this brought a smile to Nothing's eyes and she loosened up a bit. Her shoe touched my feet for a brief second and she could have sworn it was unintentional. I felt a cry inside me wanting to jump out of my chest.

"Do you do this often?" she asked me, tossing her head sideways.

"Do this?"

"You know, inviting people over like that."

"Never," Kamru mumbled into his food, "never ever."

"Then I must feel special. Eh, Uncle? Anything you have in mind? I once knew this guy who kept following me around being nice to me and all. And when I asked him why, he said he liked my...can you guess what?"

I kept quiet. Kamru asked, "What?"

"The hair on my chin. You know, I had this long hair on the mole somewhere here," she laughed pointing to the spot. Kamru too, found that amusing. "So I cut the nuisance and gave it to him, and he actually disappeared from my life."

She shrieked even louder and I waited for her to quieten down before I asked Nothing in the earnestness of shears talking to sheep, "What do you think I want from you, now that the hair is gone?"

The air became sombre again. But when I asked a question I wanted an answer, and silence was no answer. I waited, looking straight at Nothing avoiding my gaze.

"Yeah?" I prompted.

"You tell me," she barely uttered.

"I think, I want you to be my wife."

Things were different after dinner. No one spoke a word since I broke the news. Death hung in the air as a wooden plank would. Kamru fidgeted around keeping an eye on both of us. In a second his existence was at the precipice. The very girl he had been rolling about with, like the hyena he was, was about to eat into his carcass. He made sounds of appearing casual. I told him to scoot to the corner shop when I couldn't stand his overacting anymore.

Even the chairs knew why he was being asked to

slink out, making it but obvious for me to not keep the lady waiting awkwardly at the table. Her lower jaw was showing off its muscles by clenching and unclenching in the manner of masticating cows. I have known people to chew gum when they were calculating and by the ferocity of her movements, she was in the thick of deep mathematical turmoil. I decided then to relieve her from the terminal fight between greed for my wealth and her youth.

"So?"

"I'm sorry," she stuttered.

"You have the entire night to decide," I smiled a one-eighth moon.

"I cannot, will not."

"This is not what I wish to hear," I said with utter calm, though my hands shook behind my back. A breath of breeze brought her smell in short gulps, scraping my bones. I could see the argument slipping out. The pain under my shirt was pinching me somewhere near the third button. I undid the first two.

She looked up. She wasn't scared no more. In fact, she had the answer written on her face. It was her turn.

"Why don't I make you happy the entire night, Uncle?"

"Eventually, yes."

"I meant exactly now."

"I don't sleep with whores," I looked straight

into her eyes, "you will have to marry me."

"I refuse. What if I refuse?"

I was thinking of an answer where there was none. Her odour began erasing whatever logic I may have stored away. *A pounding inside became longer and louder. I heard a glass-pane shatter in my eyes. Everything turned frosty. I felt the hair on my arms rise as a cold wave ran through me.* And suddenly I saw Nothing again.

She stood behind her chair tightly clutching a large serving spoon - yellow with gravy - that dripped between her fingers. I told her to sit down. She believed in the spoon more than she trusted my words.

"Sit down," I spoke firmly.

She had the nerve to say, "You're mad. I shouldn't have stayed back. I'll call my people. I'll, I'll hit you. Please." And she sat down. "What do you want from me? Why me? Just look at me. Look. Look." She opened her shirt and pulled out her pear-sized breasts. "Look. What is there to look? Why me?" She started wailing.

I heard a headache knock on me. "Will you cut it and give it to me?" I pointed to her chest, "Will you? I'm the boy chasing you."

"I didn't mean it that way," she whimpered.

"Will you give it to me or not?"

"I'm sorry, Uncle, I'm sorry."

"Yes or no?"

"No, please, no," she was overdoing it. Her voice was going out the open front door and down the road. Kamru never crossed my mind. "I know I'm a whore," she wailed, "I'm a bad whore."

"Do you want to give up?"

"Yes. Yes," she came up behind me and put her hand on my neck. Her odour swam around me. *My eyes glazed over again. I heard the sound of water splashing, a steel bucket kicked across the floor. A pair of hands was rubbing my neck and back. A smell of soap was all over me.*

"Then marry me, Nina," I groaned.

Nothing jumped back.

# *Chapter 16*

Nothing knew something - that I could never hurt her. Her door remained ajar in the night. She had given away all her womanly possessions night after night and whatever she had to lose was safe inside the ribcage of a man nearly three times her age. Your emotions always belong to someone else. I learned a new truth about myself and it made me feel angry after all these years. There were so many forgotten feelings coming back to me. I realized that even a prostitute had a choice and I wasn't it. I had become a teenager at sixty-something.

Eleven times in the night, I walked past her door, waited outside and sitting at the edge of her bed watched her sleep. She stirred too often in unannounced spasms of violence. Her cover had been flung off, her shirt buttons were undone and her plain cotton petticoat had climbed up beyond her knee. I had the feeling she was watching me too. Her breathing would hold for a moment too long when I brought my face close to her. Her soapy smell mixed with sweat lingered around the room in little explosions in the air. She scratched her thighs and her arms and, when some confusion entered her dream, she scratched her hair in an audible manner of midnight mice. Tiny specks of black decorated her pillow and I knew at once what they were. Lice.

Twice Kamru shouted in his sleep. He had hung his rats on Emarti's picture in the Vulture Room after boiling them on a string for an hour. He did this every Tuesday for peace, he lied. I knew well that it was to get rid of the girl. The peculiar aroma, of a dog wet in the rain, floated half-way up the stairs filling me with an air of unpleasantness.

I caught Nothing looking at me through a chink. She had no time to pretend, so she opened her eyes wide. Her hands did not pull back the clothes; instead the breast I had been acquainted with tumbled out. She spread her legs as a laboratory rat pinned to wax. I got up with a creak.

"What if I said yes," she drawled. She was drunk. "What will it satisfy?" I made my way to the door and shut it. "I am giving you all that a man wants and you want to marry me. I'm ugly. I'm sick." I went back to the edge of the bed. "I'm a whore because I'm ugly. No one will ever want me." I took her limp hand in mine. "Do you see the beauty within?" I was about to say 'yes' when she started laughing at me. "Once you marry me, you'll start seeing the ugliness inside, Uncle." Her tirade tired her out and her head fell to one side, asleep.

That I hadn't spoken a word made my head want to burst. I went looking for Kamru to relieve the bubble in my brain. He wasn't there in his room. I found the main door open. I had to scout around for the slimy medicine myself - I saw it sitting still, flicking its tongue on a corner stool. I picked up a shoe and beat the house gecko to a yellow-reddish pulp.

Kamru's method of meditation calmed me down. Slowly, the throbbing subsided. I pulled a chair close to the front door and waited for the dog's return from a hole in the night.

I don't know when I dropped off. A hinge whined me awake. Kamru stood over me. He held a small newspaper packet between his fingers. The wall-clock said three-fifteen.

Before I opened my mouth, he said, "The girl won't let you sleep?"

I nodded.

"Want me to?"

I shook my head not asking what he wanted to do.

"Nina?"

I nodded.

"Tch."

I shrugged my shoulders. The newspaper packet in Kamru's hand was shedding fresh red juice. I never did go too much into his personal space unless it affected me. Some people preserved leaves plucked off plants between leaves of a book. He collected fingers. I just didn't like him mothering me.

He disappeared into his room. I waited at the door. There was a slight shuffle on the stairs. Nothing came down dressed in her glossy business suit. She hadn't washed her face.

"Be going, Uncle."

I nodded.

She left the door slightly open and went away, unafraid of the dark. A stray dog filled the slit she left behind and complained.

# *Chapter 17*

Bidiya called up to say everything was fine. Without telling Kamru where I was going or warning Bidiya that I was coming, I took the night train to Didoli. I trusted both of them, yes, but this thing called trust, in my world, was made of iron and not ceramic; it didn't shatter but was prone to slowly surely rust. It was a quiet cat on my lap and not a growling dog lounging on the floor. But when my cat says all is fine, I smell a boiled rat the size of a dog.

I thought a lot about Nothing. Had she died I would not have wept, but knowing she was out there smelling like Nina after a bath pulled at a hair in my armpit, hurting me. It was obvious she would not be making an appearance at the house again. I decided to hunt for her the day I got back.

Early next morning, I knocked on the glass pane fogged by my breath. I could see the shape of Bidiya moving about inside. I knocked sharper this time. The shape came towards the door. After a brief struggle the lock clicked. I stood face to face with a man of white descent.

"Yes?" he said.

"Is my wife at home?" I asked gently.

The only other time I saw colour drain from flesh so fast was in death by dagger. The sight of a toothy blade does half the trick and the stabbing kind of pulls the plug. I saw Emarti's final complexion reflect in the gentleman's cheeks.

"May I speak with my wife?"

"You mean," he faltered.

"Yes," I stepped past him a little more firmly. He waited where he stood, unsure of which way to move. I could see his trekker's bag and bicycle piled atop each other. Bidiya came out of the bedroom drying her hair. If the loudest scream is the silent one then this was it.

I took her by the elbow, "Nice place you have here, Ma'am. Do we get tea?"

"Yes," she was nervous, "of course."

"Call your friend inside. Why is he holding up the wall? He stayed the night, I suppose. I wonder where he slept. Nina's bed, hmmm?"

Bidiya cleared the bed of all her things and some books and music that I assumed belonged to her stranger. I went straight to the bathroom. Steam from a recent bath hung in the air with memories of Nina rubbing soap on my back. Bidiya's own stuff was hung about in the manner becoming a regular whore. My expectations, I agreed, were too high. I hit the flush to warn her I was coming out.

She had hurriedly tidied up the room and was sitting by the window with two cups of tea, not three.

"Where's the third?" I smiled casually.

"He has to leave."

"Call him."

Bidiya hesitated.

"Call him," I hissed.

She came back with the man. He hadn't recovered. I walked up to him with an extended cup.

"I was hoping you would share tea with me before you left. Bidiya, get yourself another."

"I know I'm intruding," he ventured reluctantly.

He relaxed when I said, "That you are, but it's alright now. You are a guest and we allow a guest five human errors. Did you sleep well?"

He looked slightly at Bidiya and rubbed his stubble, "Thank you. Yes. After a month. Been riding, you see."

"I can see that," I said. "Did Bidiya take good care?"

"Oh, yes."

"And have you paid her?"

"I mean to. Frankly, you took me by surprise," he managed a laugh. He was happy she wasn't my wife.

I too started laughing. Bidiya was biting her

nails.

"Let me make up for the shock," I said, "stay the night."

Bidiya's eyes went wide. She tried to warn the white to stay away and he was looking at the generosity in my eyes.

"Get your stuff back in," I told him. And when he was gone, I turned to Bidiya, "Big mistake?"

She was suddenly braver, "We all make mistakes."

"All?"

"I haven't asked him to marry me. Like some people."

It took me a while to figure out where she was coming from. Bidiya had sent Nothing. Nothing had told her everything.

"Word has gone around," she carried on, "the girls are wary of an old man who won't lay off. Big mistake, Uncle."

I sat silently chewing an idea. Here was someone who would tell me where to find Nothing or whatever her name was. All she needed was my kind of gentle coercion and I knew exactly to what degree. The white man was a godsend from the devil.

Evening came. I called up Kamru twice informing him I was on my way and he should expect me in the night. He didn't ask where I was and it suited me fine. There was a piece of news he said he must give me in person for he feared someone could listen-in on the phone. I told him to stop scaring me. We both laughed. Mason, for that was the white man's name, squeezed my left shoulder imagining I was in good spirits. My right hand fondled the flip-open shaving razor in my jacket pocket.

"I am a good masseur," I said cradling the phone.

"Yeah?" he sounded a bit wary. I got the feeling Bidiya had warned him about my turns of temper, though in no way could she have told him what to expect.

I brought out my razor.

"With a blade? Massage with a blade?" his tone was trying to sound intrigued.

"Are you afraid? You've been cycling for a month. You must have seen a lot of this stuff." I was talking plain. "It's yours."

Mason stopped smiling, "You've been through my things. I should have known. What else have you taken?"

"This," I held up a finger. He shrugged. Bidiya showed up.

"Dinner," she said.

I shut the razor and slapped Mason's back. He barely managed an expression.

"Scared you? Let's eat," I led the way to Nina's table.

Mason hesitated. I started serving. Bidiya, I realized, was a disaster management cook. The kind for whom taste is decided by the level of hunger at the shelter. I made a face and that made Mason smile. He had suffered her cooking on many an occasion or so it seemed. He pulled a chair and sat down to the torture.

Bidiya sat across and bit her lip in anticipation of what, I guess, even she didn't know.

Nina's wall-clock struck a long noisy eight. I looked around the house full of her things. *I felt the urge to lie down. Nina was saying something to me. She was telling me to go have a bath before supper. I walked over to the couch. I could feel her eyes upon me. I lay down with my back to her. A warmth engulfed me. I liked the sounds of the night outside. Her right hand crept under my filthy shirt and rubbed my right nipple.* I felt a larger hand on my arm. Mason was looking gravely at me.

"All fine?" he asked.

It took me some time to answer. The ringing of the chime in my ear died down. I told him to come closer. He bent his head lower. I sliced open his neck with his own razor. Bidiya once again uttered the most silent scream in the world. I saw her slip and settle down at the base of the wall with her eyes and mouth and legs wide open.

Meanwhile, Mason was a thrashing chicken on the floor. He became still. His colour turned the whitest of white.

"Big mistake," I looked at Bidiya.

"What will I do now?" she quivered.

"Get rid of the body."

"How?" she asked after many moments elapsed.

"Find a way," I spoke like a boss, "I can't keep doing your dirty work for you." And I lopped off Mason's middle finger to ensure Bidiya's unadulterated cooperation.

In an hour I was on my way to Kamru. In my hand was Nothing's everything I needed to know.

# *Chapter 18*

So, I called up Nothing many days after I had promised myself. Naturally, she was disturbed. I tried to explain why it was important that we meet and she began yelling at me. I was running on low self-respect and it made emotions easier to bear. Kamru had been moody of late and I sent him on an errand out of town merely to cheer myself up. I never told him Nothing's real name: Zila.

I was beginning to lose sleep. It became imperative to manage the ravages of my conflicts within. Zila was making things somewhat sharper for both of us. I had long forgotten how to take a 'no' and her shrieks over the phone left many 'hellos' unanswered. Had she been kinder, I would have been calmer, but loose ends are loose ends, and they are invariably plugged-in at the other end with a finger on the switch. Her scent made me shiver, and the thought of her was a pleasant nightmare I was now determined to end.

Kamru informed me he was in a town called

Chindi and had bought the bottles as I'd instructed. I said I was pleased and he must enjoy himself as much as he deserved. He must, however, take the first bus home after the dark and the deed were done. He wanted to stay on for a few days more, so I let him. And got down to tie my own wires neatly.

I dialled. The voice at the other end wanted to ask my entire history and geography. I told him to get Zila on the line or I wouldn't hesitate in saying things about his mother.

"Now what, Uncle," Zila took the phone, "I think I told you where to go."

I swallowed a lump and gave myself a deep breath before I said, "I only called to say goodbye."

"Well goodbye then," she sounded relieved and that hurt me.

"Though I still wish you marry me. I may die in a couple of years and all this could be yours."

"I don't want you dead, Uncle, I just want you gone. There are some nice things about you."

That made me feel better. I went on, "Like what?"

"Now you're being greedy," she said.

I liked this. "Tell me. What's nice about an old rat?" I asked.

She thought for a while and said, "You are kind of gentlemanly. You treat women well." There was a long silence, which translated into impatience. Was she making faces at her companion? Without warning she asked, "Do I remind you of someone?"

"Yes. My best friend. She's dead."

"I'm sorry. What of her?"

"I have no idea. It's a presence, I believe."

"That's vague, don't you think?"

"You smell like her."

"The problem is," she said, "you want her, not me. If I change my soap, I'll be someone else."

"It's not the soap," I was again bargaining. She waited for a 'then what'. "It's your sweaty armpits, and something I can't put together."

"Well, I never," she broke off.

"Won't you visit me?" I was sobbing inside.

"Can't promise, Uncle. Goodbye."

I stood still in my room with the phone hanging from my hand. Moisture condensed in my eyes. The bell for Room 8 rang shrill. I rushed to open the door. The couple glanced at each other.

"All well, Uncle?" the man put a hand on my shoulder.

I took the money and waved them away.

The phone rang a half hour later. It was Kamru.

"Done," he said. I calmed down considerably.

Two days later, Kamru came home looking pleased. A month after that, late in the night, there was a knock on the door. It opened to a woman wrapped in a black sheet so completely that only her half-shut eyes showed. She stood there twinkling her tears at me. I waited for her storm to subside.

At last a strangled voice cried out, "They are all bastards, Uncle. They are all filthy bastards." She broke down. I led her inside by the elbow. Kamru pulled out a chair for her at the dining table and we sat to kill the cat.

"I'm finished, Uncle," Zila spoke through her shroud. Kamru's eyes widened. "No one wants me now. They have all run away. My business is doomed. I remembered your words, so I came. You can ask me to go away and I will."

Having no time for circus, I asked, "What happened?"

She uncovered a bit of her face below the eyes. "What happened to your nose?" Kamru exclaimed at the two holes on her stretched skin, "Leprosy?" He pushed back his chair an inch.

"See what I mean?" Zila pulled up the sheet again. "No, it's not that, maybe worse. This is the closest I've come to anyone in weeks."

I cleared my throat, "When did this happen?"

"A month. Have been in hospital ever since. All alone. They ate up my savings trying to save me. I'm still in pain, Uncle. And half-blind. I just came to ask you one simple question."

"Ask," I said.

"Will you let me live with you? I'm not asking for anything more. Will you?" I kept silent and she gathered herself to get up. I put a light hand on her shoulder.

"I am tired of kind words," she sounded exhausted, "if you cannot answer yes or no, I'll go at once."

"What if I let you stay?" I was talking to the hand I held. I felt a drop fall on mine. She was at it again. Kamru was staring at me. I repeated my question.

"I'll become invisible. I'll do everything."

"What if I hurt your friends?"

"They are not my friends."

"What if I hurt them?"

"Whatever you say," her eyes lighted up, "I'll be your slave."

"Will you marry me then?"

Kamru's chair toppled. He was standing up glaring at us. His sacrifice of eleven rats and a baby-finger had backfired. I glared back and he settled down again. Zila was holding my hand tighter, but I believe in the clarity of words.

"Will you marry me?"

"Yes," she said, "but won't you first look at me fully? You may change your mind." And with that she pulled the black sheet off. Kamru gasped. I was taken aback five paces more than I expected. We saw before us an embarrassed monster.

Zila had no face. It was as if a kid had wiped the wall clean. Her skin had been boiled in hot water for a week, and stretched like a drum. Bloody sores oozed down to her neck and maybe deeper.

She wore an orange antiseptic generously. Her eyes had shrunken to nothing. Her hair, most of it, had been burnt to a greyish-white curly mass.

"Fire?" Kamru cleared his throat.

"Worse," she said quietly.

"What could be worse?" Kamru looked at me for an answer. I shrugged my shoulder. He turned to her.

Zila whispered, "Acid."

"Who?" Kamru asked and then added, "why?"

She hadn't a clue. "Some guy on a bicycle in the dark. His face was covered. He came from behind and poured it on my head from a bottle. I woke up on the street the next morning and walked home feeling the way with my hands."

"Where?" Kamru was barely audible.

"Chindi," she said, "where I lived. Don't I look terrible?"

"I don't care how you look. You still smell the same," I smiled.

## *Chapter 19*

We married amongst funeral ashes in the cremation ground on the seashore, just outside the city. Kamru was there and so was Bidiya and they insisted on a custom wherein a whore must wed the dead before tying a mortal knot. It was a way, they said, of not letting the bride go back to her old meandering habits. The spirits of the dead took root inside her if she as much as tried thinking of escape. I was merely the third person in the transaction. Now, the only other male relation from the nether I was aware of was my father, and Zila was told to marry him before she was allowed to be mine. I did all that I could to get her and here she was…first being wed to my father's ghost, I laughed at my fate. Between all forms of Nina and I, there stood Father in all his heavenly glory. Once again I was the stepson, a step away from possessing a woman absolutely.

I wanted to tell them all this was unnecessary because Zila's current looks could scare off any loitering ghost, but I held my tongue. A eunuch with a manly chant and in a woman's petticoat performed the rites. Ari arrived drunk and what she murmured made sense under the circumstances. We were made to bite off a piece of flesh and asked to wash it down with liquor from a round earthen pot. Only later was I told it was the half-burnt remains of a human and I was now officially ordained in the profession. In my death, Zila had a right over every little I owned. Kamru and Bidiya, the witnesses, had cause for silence.

I took them aside one by one and told them how much I distrusted silence and if they chose to remain so, I would have their tongues sacrificed for a purpose. On the other hand, I told them, there were expansion plans that would put our present business to shame.

Just then, in the manner of a poet, I was struck by two thoughts: a mammoth idea, which would unfold much later; and a lesser, more moderate one, which came into effect immediately after the wedding. I needed to recruit urgently. While Kamru, Bidiya and my new wife sashayed towards the house in a state of euphoria, I was already home pouring over the first draft of my lesser brainwave - the Boredom-Bedroom Project.

The idea was simple, obviously inspired by Zila. If a whore could become an irreversible housewife, a wife of many years could become a professional too. Any woman of forty and over was hungry and should leap at a juicy one thrown at her. Her husband of many years was probably already hunting in the neighbourhood, in his mind at least. This was an opportunity waiting to be devoured.

Kamru was the key to my current clockwork, Bidiya managed the night traffic and so it was natural that Zila handled the new business. The moment the three made an incoherent appearance at the doorstep, I put them to bed and decided to sleep over my rough outline. The day had been declared a holiday by the board of drunkards, though duties would resume at ten in the night. I sat near Zila's burnt head and bathed in her Ninaness.

"You may call me Nina if you like," she murmured. I just looked at her and considered my luck. Marriage had not made her thankless even in delirium.

"Thank you," she drawled again, "Uncle."

I felt an urge of a forty-year-old woman rise up inside me. Zila's expressionless face filled me with affection. I lay down beside her and slipped my hands into the space between her skin and silk. It did not occur to me then how odd a purveyor of emotions would find the ritual of the bed. I counted, Zila called me 'Uncle' five times in the next half-hour. I made love for the first time since I married Emarti.

When I woke up, the bell was ringing angrily. Zila was looking at herself in the mirror. And by the sound of it, Kamru had released the people in Room 7. My headthrob pounded my eyes. I pulled myself away from the sheets.

"Happy, Uncle?" Zila's reflection glanced at me.

"Yes," I said, "and be pleased to know your friends in Chindi will be here shortly.

"I don't want," she sounded annoyed.

"Yes you will."

She turned her back to me. I shouted for Kamru, and Bidiya turned up. Kamru was throwing up in the sea, she informed us with a sly smile which clearly meant she was getting comfortable in the environment at the house. Didoli was too quiet for the creature gnawing at her spirit.

"Get the wooden box from the cabinet under the stairs," I ordered her sternly. She went off with a toss of her head. "The one that came in last Thursday," I called after her.

Zila turned and cast a question mark at me.

"A wedding gift," I said. She walked across the bed on her knees and came towards me. Her face was so stretched I could not tell her feelings. There was slight moisture at the corner of an eye making me infer she was emotional. She shocked me completely by hopping onto my lap and putting her arms around my neck. When Bidiya returned with the box, Zila was asleep on my shoulder, a thumb in her mouth. Bidiya couldn't hide her contempt as she handed me Mason's shaving razor to cut open the binds.

"Cute," she told the walls and swept out.

Zila opened her eyes a bit of all she could. "Bidiya is jealous," she whispered, "and Kamru is angry. Be careful."

I nodded. After twenty years someone was telling me to take care of myself. I shook with a fever difficult to explain.

"I will, Nina," I said involuntarily.

Zila smiled broadly, "I like being her."

"Here, open this," I pushed the box towards her.

Predictably, she asked, "What's in it? I'm jumping inside me. Does anyone know?"

I shook my head, "Show me."

She tore open the secret with her painted nails and gawked at the entrails. Her hand went to her mouth.

"I promised you," I explained, "your friends from Chindi. They will always be yours."

She seemed too overwhelmed with the gesture. Her eyes half-wide.

"Like it?" I smiled.

"Teeth?" she said.

"Four friends. Forty teeth. Took a day. Like it?"

She nodded slowly and broke into a broad grin. I felt relieved my gift was accepted.

"Want to be a businesswoman?" I asked before she recovered.

"What business do I know?" she laughed.

"The only one you know now," I prompted.

"Housewife?"

# *Chapter 20*

This is how it worked.

Zila called up a random number and asked for the lady of the house. If the wife was between forty and fifty, she came to the point.

"Want a college boy to drive you around when your husband is out of town?"

One out of the six called, angrily whispered 'yes'. Zila had two hundred subscribers in the first quarter. There were rules, of course.

The service was for the day only.

The car belonged to the service.

The identity of the driver and the driven was a code.

Payment was made at booking time.

Leaving the city was prohibited.

There was no subscription fee.

Food was not included.

It was necessary to keep replenishing the numbers because one out of three drivers and the driven drove away from the service provider.

The cars belonged to the young men looking for fun for which they too paid a fee. Zila merely brought the needy together. The money wasn't good, it was great. The pleasure was phenomenal. Car sales went up.

Just when we thought we had a business school case-study, Zila vomited boiled cabbage. The doctors told her to take it easy. She became a vegetable. The service vanished overnight.

But this wasn't the mammoth idea I had in the cremation ground. As I said earlier, that was to develop and come into this world many months later.

Meanwhile, Zila bloated up. Bidiya came over from Didoli to tell me I was distracted. Kamru's room yielded fingers off and on. Bidiya went back licking her envy. I told Kamru to get rid of the child, which was not meant to happen. It was the fourth month. We took Zila to the temple of the altar and left her there the whole night. She disappeared.

"What do you mean?" I collared Kamru.

"She ran away," he said.

"Where could she?"

"Chindi."

"No," my senses said Kamru was drawing me away from the truth, "she is hiding within five miles of the house." I saw Kamru stare at the sky uncomfortably.

"Is it your child?" I pushed him.

"You're mad," he said.

"Then let me handle this."

He took me to a small house in the neighbourhood. Zila looked at us without a word, she started screaming. I took her in my arms. She quietened down. I sat down on the cot and told Kamru to wait outside. Zila came and sat on my lap. She put her thumb in her mouth. She had become much heavier since the wedding. She smelled the same. She fell asleep the same way.

"Let's go home," I said.

"And the child?" she opened her eyes.

"Goes with us."

"How far?" Kamru prodded on the way home.

"Till birth at least."

No one, including me, knew what that meant.

"What happens if you feel the urge again?" Kamru whispered matter-of-factly.

"Kill something at the altar," I replied. He was happy.

One afternoon, as a very fat housemaid massaged Zila's swollen legs, the phone rang next to her. A woman's voice asked if she was so-and-so and when Zila said she was, the caller asked her age.

I heard Zila joke, "I'm old enough for anything you may want to sell. Even a blue elephant." She was talking so loud, I was sure she was playing to our ears. But what she heard next made her drop the phone.

"She doesn't have a blue elephant?" I laughed.

Zila kept silent indicating someone had insulted her.

"Tell me," I called out and requested the fat lady to leave us alone.

"The woman asked me if I needed a young man to drive me around town when my husband was out," she said in a shaky voice.

"So?"

"That was my line."

"I know," I pursed my lips.

"Someone stole my business."

"Money doesn't keep waiting," I explained with growing impatience.

"Has to be someone we know."

I didn't inform her just then that I don't easily let go of an advantage and, I had this widow in her thirties manage the Boredom-Bedroom Project when Zila, so conveniently, chose to get pregnant. I didn't tell anyone that I trusted a woman who had slaughtered her husband with a shard of mirror – and spent twelve years in prison – to handle my own baby lovingly. Like I said, for me trust wasn't a porcelain cup that broke easily, it was an iron mug that would eventually rust.

"Her name was Daya," Zila said.

"Sounds familiar," I replied and walked off to tell Kamru to kill a goat because I was feeling a bit distressed. Daya had no business calling up my number and giving away her name. She was either too clever or too stupid.

# *Chapter 21*

The day was coming closer. My ribs were getting tighter. Once, on a quiet evening, we sat around the dining table with our chairs pushed back. Zila had plonked down with her legs thrown out, holding her rotundity between her palms. The calm on her lips seemed to affect me. I expected, within days, news good enough to clobber my head and couldn't explain the feeling of doom sitting round the corner.

A dull hammering went on in a room out there. *Rice was on the boil somewhere. A sharp pain twanged my left earlobe. A helplessness grew out of the walls around me. I heard voices and music of a teary nature. The pain was not inside the ear, but on the worthless hanging mass of skin itself.*

"You okay, Boss?" Kamru interrupted, "you look all red."

"Can you stop the hammering?" I asked.

He looked at Zila and they both kneeled down beside me. Zila touched my cheek and I winced.

*The pain was unbearable.* I held my ears.

"Can't you stop the hammering?" I cried.

"What hammering, Boss?"

"My ears are bleeding, you dog, get me hot water. And tell those guys to stop the banging." I said a lot of things I don't remember, though Kamru kept reminding me for a year of how I was calling my mother a whore; I would yell at her to stop hurting me. But I had no reason to believe a man I had tamed instead of keeping a mongrel, and when Zila seconded his words, I distrusted her just as much.

"You have no right to call my mother-in-law names," she gurgled happily while I lay bathed in sweat many minutes later.

"You had an attack," she stroked my head, "just relax."

I said, seemingly out of context and partly to change the subject, "I want your child dead. I can't rest. How will you compensate?"

She looked at me as if she didn't believe me.

"We've sacrificed fourteen goats already to keep you cool. What more do you want?" Kamru spoke for her, heightening my bitterness.

"Why does it not appease the gods?" I held his elbow and shook it hard.

"What more do you want, Boss?"

"A child for a child," I said.

Kamru didn't utter another word. He walked

out of the front door. I was sure he got what 'a child for a child' meant.

The only equivalent of birth was death or, in this case, sacrifice. Only a newborn has the unadulterated power of the unknown, Nina had said, as it was closest to creation and, therefore, perfection. An offering of fourteen goats or twenty cows or a busload of fully-grown men dare not come close to the freshly-drawn blood of a pink-fleshed baby. The indecipherable baby-cry pierces the eardrum of the sky and changes fortunes. Anything else was just plain less. Days dulled the bloody devils and years diluted their darkness. And in extreme situations, just any just-born was just not enough - it had to be a girl. It had to be a girl because only she had the ultimate potential to create life. Her sacrifice was 'the' sacrifice. And if she was the pain, then only she was the antidote, Kamru knew that. Only a girl-child could match a girl-child.

Zila was staring at her navel. Moments later and days too soon, propelled by my words her head jerked back. She spread her legs wider. I locked the house. She had sunk down on the carpet.

"Don't worry, I'm there," I said, surprised by my own concern. I pulled a sheet over her, glad it was the day off.

"No, not you," she protested feebly, "I want a doctor."

"Just relax," I whispered, "it's only a child attack. We'll have him in minutes."

"Her. Don't hurt her," she begged.

There was no time to call the midwife. There was no way of calling back Kamru. I had sent the fat lady away. *The doom round the corner was sitting on the carpet in my living room. The hammering had begun again.* I tried to focus.

"Help, help," Zila yelped. *The noise got louder.* I shut my ears with cushions from the dining chairs. She pushed herself away across the floor. I reached out to soothe her excitement. She bit me on the hand. I pulled her back on the carpet and held her down. *A hundred bees were stinging my ears.* Her eyes bulged out dangerously. My head was spinning in all directions. I think I collapsed.

Kamru had not returned. I turned my head to see where I was. On the floor, Zila lay sprawled across the mess. There was no one around. I did not hear a baby's cry.

I sat up with difficulty. Zila was breathing and blowing tiny bubbles at the mouth. I crawled over to her and lifted her head into my lap. She opened her eyes slowly.

"You killed her?" she asked.

I looked into her eyes, "Who?"

She started gathering her petticoat up at the waist. A ruddy mass of flesh lay entangled in a bigger bloody mishmash.

"She's dead?" Zila looked into me.

I said, "Correct."

A soft knocking became fiercer when we didn't get up to open the door. I heard Kamru shouting in a hoarse whisper. I wanted to collect what he was saying so I trudged to the door. I saw Zila refusing to move and walked back to pull down her clothes. Kamru was calling with some urgency. I opened the door to him holding a newborn, the way Sattu had in Didoli the first time I saw him.

"A child for a child," he said.

I told him what had happened and why there was no need for sacrifice.

"I went all the way, Boss," he whined.

I said I was sorry it was all over. The gods were satisfied and he must return the girl to the mother.

"I'll keep her," I heard Zila groan. She was looking at both of us with her expressionless face, "A child for a child." After all this, she still had the presence for twisting Nina's phrase to her advantage. The idea of equating a living child with a dead one did not appeal to me in the least. She was deliberately sacrificing my peace.

I struck Kamru across the chin.

I was okay with the girl, she wasn't mine. Neither did she have Nina's smell. However, she made a peculiar sound at times that brought a burnt flavour to my tongue, like licking a pot of charred milk. I spat when she did that.

"Let's name her Nina," Zila tried her luck very casually while the baby sucked. I wasn't falling for that one.

"We have a custom in the family," I changed the subject a fraction of an inch, "we could follow it or not. Your choice."

"Of course," she went on being nice, "we must. Nina needs to grow on values."

"We can't call her Nina. The girl needs another." My abruptness lay to rest all sounds of protest.

"And the tradition?" she ventured after a while.

"A bit painful it was for me. But my mother wanted it."

"Like a tattoo," she smiled understandingly.

"Somewhat. I'll need nails and a hammer and fourteen yellow marigolds. You'll need to cook sweetened rice."

"Now?" Her enthusiasm dipped a bit.

There were six guests in the house and Kamru could handle the lot on his own. I said, "Yeah, it's Tuesday. Perfect." She got up inch-by-inch like a car-jack. "And by the way," I added, "Mother performed the ceremony." Zila walked to the kitchen doubtfully eating her defaced lips.

I went looking for the hammer and six inch nails I had stashed away in a storage space under the stairs. Fresh marigold I borrowed from the garland on Emarti's picture in the Vulture Room. I could hear Zila clanking away in the kitchen and Kamru talked to her in whispers. A louder 'but' or 'I know' or 'how should I know' gave me to derive she was jittery. I waited for them to make an entry together. The girl slept appropriately in a large basket meant for potatoes. Relaxed, I too gently wafted off into a trance distant sounds bring. A lazy melody I'd heard in my childhood hung above my head. I hummed snatches of it, sitting back, eyes closed.

*The smell of saffron danced in the air. I heard my mother singing the same village song she sang in the bath, a popular song in those days.* I slobbered a few words from here and there. My dribble cooled my chin. *The carpenter's idiot-apprentice was knocking on a new cabinet for the radio. I floated away from my nursery books with large pictures of animals dressed like people, and found myself standing over a bowl of sweetened rice sitting and steaming on the kitchen slab. In the background, the boy's hammer went thak-thak-thak-thak absent-mindedly.*

*I put my fingers in the slimy sticky rice, made a small ball and chucked it into my mouth. I chewed and swallowed in rhythm with the hammering far away. Clumsily my hands slipped and knocked the bowl off the edge, and soon Mother stood panting over me. I saw her seized by a witch once again. She often took her venom out on me, for no real reason. She dragged me by the collar to where the idiot was playing with tools I wasn't allowed to touch. My head was pushed to the top of the wooden cabinet. I tried to run because this was someone else boiling inside her in scalding oil. Mother slapped me a hundred thousand times till I saw the room spinning faster than my eyes could catch. She pushed my head down on the cabinet one last time. I stayed still lest I got another round.*

*A sharp pain stung my left ear. Mother held my face down hurting my nose. A deadlier stab went through my right ear. I could barely breathe. Mother had nailed my ears to the top of the new radio cabinet. The apprentice ran out of the house howling. Mother made herself a cup of tea. I fainted.*

"Here's your sweetened rice," Zila was shaking me. My shirt stuck to my back with wetness. It took me a while to take in the scene. At last, I pulled myself up in the armchair. The girl was still fast asleep in the vegetable basket.

"Bring her here," I ordered. Zila obeyed. "Put her face down on the table." She did. "Put the flowers around her head." Kamru did that. I handed Zila the hammer and the nails.

"Now?" She was scared. Kamru stood watching.

"Hammer the nails into the girl's ears exactly as my mother did," I said quietly.

"What is this?" Zila screamed.

"Nail her ears to the table."

"But why?" she exclaimed.

I told her, "A child for a child."

Zila kept screaming.

Kamru somehow understood what made me detest the idea of a child in the house in the first place; he remained unperturbed to my outbursts. The mad memories of my childhood were already difficult to kill. And now, it seemed, only the pain of a child could possibly kill the pain of my childhood. This was Nina's school of thought to which we both belonged.

The banshee cries still belonged to Zila.

# *Chapter 22*

The girl turned two. When I felt a bit affectionate I called her Kutti or bitch, otherwise she had no name I was aware of. Zila had assured me by slitting her wrists twice that she never contemplated running away and she was still grateful to me for letting her feed the bitch in her infancy. I saw no connection between milk and motherhood except that, at least in my case, both boiled over without warning.

"It's my blood," Zila said theatrically, propagating this was what blood relations actually meant. I curtailed her going to the movies on the weekends to teach her a slice of reality. She started spending all her time with the girl to spite me and I put my mind in the business.

Bidiya had grown in her capacity in ways I'll soon explain. Daya worked in the shadows as before though even her slight change of mood made car dealers sweat. She wanted a house of her own to manage and, naturally, she turned to me. I could not handle all of Bidiya's traffic and so diverted a good chunk of it to Daya. Kamru had the nights planned differently for over a year. We diversified into a hugely unrelated area of which I had an inkling on the day of my wedding to Zila in the cremation ground. This was our monster pleasure, the mammoth idea, and it translated into substantial gains. Actually, I was only taking Nina's work forward.

Kutti started it all. The need for babies sprung upon me the day Kamru brought her home. He had a way with newborns. They were lighter, unrecognized and, in most cases, unwanted if they happened to be girls, which was perfect for the business we were evolving to: of sacrifice.

Kamru was looking for a sign it seemed, and Kutti's arrival brought him back into his original form. He stood swaying over my head one hazy afternoon.

"Someone wants to sacrifice a child for a child," he grinned.

I thought he was mocking me and told him to go play games with Zila in the kitchen.

"Someone wants a baby, Boss," he kept grinning.

"Then tell her to occupy one of the rooms," I caught him by the belt and shook him, "and I'll send a river of bulls to mount her till she is done. Go take your fleas with you."

He went away, but I could see him pacing in his smelly room thinking of a new approach. Soon he stood over me again.

"One of Nina's old customers wants to sacrifice a baby for a baby he desperately wants his wife to have," he glared at me in great earnest. "Someone from Didoli. Bidiya sent him here with a recommendation. He wants a girl today. I can arrange."

I showed little interest even when my entrails were boiling at the coincidence. I was standing face to face with my future plan and here it was asking to be mine. Just how the idea had come to me in the first place - as an unexpected gift, inspired by the business of death amongst the funeral fires at my wedding. What could mirror the pleasure of pain at birth better than the pleasure of pain at a sacrifice! Fire eats fire, poison burns poison and pain parallels pain. A woman must sacrifice someone else's baby to give birth to her own. I smiled at the irony.

"I know," I lied, "learn to talk straight. We are running a business here, not a playschool for imbeciles."

Shamelessness had a face and it glowed at me, "Then, Boss?"

"Go do it. What do you want from me? Get down on my knees and sing devotions to you? Get out and work." He stood there like Emarti's picture holding a scowl. "Now what!"

"The party wants us to do it too."

"Didn't I just say 'do it', Moron!"

He bent a little closer and mumbled, "They want the sacrifice here. They want us to do it."

I pondered a moment. The dog began panting his onion breath, enveloping me. My original idea was to be the facilitator and not the doctor. I saw Kutti waddling towards me and things became crystal. "Okay," I snapped at the dog, "we'll do it tonight. Get the goat."

"The baby, Boss," Kamru corrected me.

I spat irritated, "We shall call it 'goat' henceforth."

Kamru wondered why and I wondered why I had let him into the house on an impulse. I had the answer later that evening.

He chose a stone slab in the centre of a barren field. A few gnarled trees stood around with us. The 'goat' had stopped crying after Kamru stuffed its mouth with his little finger. I remembered the bundle was quiet when Sattu showed it to Nina and me in Didoli. The husband of the wife who could not beget a son stood a little sideways murmuring to a man with a more confident air. A weak yellow lantern threw pale flickering shadows and gave the ceremony a gloomy feel. I was happy when Kamru drew out from a cloth bag seven earthen lamps and lit them around the slab.

"Seven is the number of teats she has," he

explained in a voice not his. "Only she can go into the past and retrieve your wishes and grant them to you."

"She?" one of us asked.

"Whose thirst do you think you are satiating with blood here?" Kamru spoke with a greater authority. Zila said milk was blood and the dog says blood is milk. The goat sucked the dog's thumb hungrily. I watched in wonder. "Lay the red cloth on the stone," he ordered.

The two strangers neatly folded a crumpled sheet to cover the slab exactly. Their hands shook.

"Now place the copper bowl in the centre of the sheet and put the sieve on top of the bowl." They did as they were guided. I felt wetness on my hand and found a scrawny dog licking it. I saw two more sitting in my shadow farther off.

Kamru asked, "Which way east?" We all gave different answers. He lay the goat down on the sieve on the bowl, which was placed on the red sheet on the stone slab, in a direction he decided was east. The goat started bawling. One of the dogs howled and stopped abruptly. Kamru called out to someone sitting on the drooping tree in a loud cry resembling anguish. He went on wailing in-between sips of very strong liquor. We all drank and banged our heads and paced up and down around the goat, who was also wailing her lungs out. Kamru told us to drop our clothes. He did too. He made us sit on all fours. He did too. The dogs were getting restless.

At last, when all we could hear was the goat's dry cry, he held out his hand.

"Give me the knife," he thundered. I threw him Mason's razor that almost always accompanied me. The men moved two paces back, probably unsure of which way the blade may fly. My head was swimming a few feet above my neck. We watched the razor touch the goat's grey-blue jugular. One of the men began weeping. I guessed it was the would-be father of a boy still unborn. Kamru sliced the neck of the pink goat and we watched it gently writhe till it became still. Blood flowed through the sieve into the bowl. We waited silently for an hour. The dogs were getting restless.

"She's heard us," Kamru said at last.

He made us dig a hole four feet deep into which he dropped the carcass, the sieve and the cloth wet in spots. We retreated a good hundred paces and studied the dogs drinking the goat's fresh red milk from the bowl.

One of the men threw up all over his companion. I couldn't help smiling in my drunkenness. The dogs were fighting, biting and quietly snarling as the bowl rattled across the stone table.

At daybreak we headed home. The men were told to bathe the to-be-born son in the same bowl. Even if they didn't, the payment had already been made. We slept like babies till the afternoon. Later on, Zila questioned what made me glance at Kutti in a certain strange way.

We had devised a system - in collaboration with city hospitals - for declaring a kicking-crying female baby a 'stillborn' - much to the convenience of the donor family as well as the recipient, who was always willing to part with a fraction of his wealth since his childless sorrow could by then only be thwarted by child sacrifice. A child for a child. Needless to say, the demand and supply matched perfectly. And in accordance with our business philosophy, we were once again the agents of pleasure with no investment whatsoever. Again, the desperation of lovers looking for a room and a manager was mirrored exactly in the eyes of customers in need of a progeny or the success of a factory. Money, like always, was an evident by-product of the entire performance. Still the business of sacrifice was quite a different kind of pleasure; it went deeper than the physical gratification bred between couples at the house. Nina would have been proud. This was indeed satisfying.

But when you lead the blind, you must also learn to think like the blind. After a year of twenty-three sacrifices, Kamru had grown arrogant to an extent and I had to domesticate him in his lair. Kutti had turned two, five weeks after she started waddling. Zila was teaching her to call me papa.

It was a Thursday night and we had a full house. I pretended to sleep on a bed full of Zila's inane rattle and a kid's cursed cries. Kamru was out playing more-important-than-thou. The bell to Room 6 rang. Zila had begun handling the visitors, as we were busier in the new enterprise. She covered her head in a dark veil before she opened the door lest she scared unsuspecting guests with her cliff face. But the bell that day wanted me to go down and ask if there was anything else needed. I motioned Zila to not budge. She grabbed the kid extra-affectionately in a display of womanly defiance. At times, I had the strong unexplainable urge to beat her with my belt - perhaps domestic thrashing was genetic after all.

I knocked on Room 6 before opening the door. Some guests invite greater respect. The man in his thirties had the swagger of a very powerful person's son and the woman on his tail wagged a finger at me like most drivers of bigger better cars than mine do on overtaking me.

"Why must you lock us in?" she demanded.

"Never mind," her partner was irritable. He had a question imprinted on his forehead; he just didn't have the juice to loosen his tongue. "I have a little dilemma," he blurted out with an effort, but to me it seemed he held a super problem.

"A nd I may have answer?" I ventured.

"We're starting the factory next month," his wife butted in. He told her to shut up. She made a face and went off for a stroll up the stairs towards my anxiety. I wanted to warn her before she crossed the landing.

The man turned to me, "We have failed once. I want to be sure this time. Any suggestions, Uncle?"

"You have all the resources. Sometimes, there are answers hidden in impossible places."

He became discreet, "Someone told me to look here."

"First ask your wife to come down," I looked him squarely, too late. A power-drill scream sent her crashing down four steps at a time. I guessed she had the fortune of chancing upon the undisguised Zila playing with her pup. The feeble lady held on to her companion's arm, making it shake. The insult in my laughter calmed her down sufficiently.

"What's there?" The man glowered at her.

"Answers," I said. Another bell rang furiously and I pushed the two back into their room as Zila released the occupants of the other room.

"She thinks she saw a ghost," chuckled Zila, coming down the stairs in her veil.

I almost told her it was an understatement as I hastened to open the couple's door to resume our conversation, but she read my thoughts and took the last jibe, "This is exactly where you saw me first. Sniffing around me for Nina's ghost, you were." She lifted up her arms, "Here, smell my step-motherly juices."

It suddenly occurred to me she had cut her wrists not for anything but in imitation of Nina's last bravado, to win my favour. *A nausea rose in my gut. I felt a raspy sandpaper brush my windpipe. Tiny worms crawled through my hair and the smell of a disinfectant filled the air. A nurse was yelling for emergency. She pulled my shirt from behind in trying to keep me off the blood that was spurting on the sheet.* A man screamed close to my ear, asking me to stop. A woman shrieked. *Dogs howled. The smell of vomited liquor soaked through everything.* I heard myself weeping.

The man and his wide-eyed wife were glaring at me. The lady spoke before thinking, "And I don't trust men who cry."

"Shut up," her husband spoke through clenched teeth.

"Then why is he crying? He was the one who scared us," she sulked. "He almost jumped at me and you know he was scary." She went and faced the window. "I'm the one to shut up in front of strange strangers," she talked to her reflection, "and why are we here in the first place? To get locked up? I'm out of here." But she stood where she stood.

Her man was relatively sane. "You fine, Uncle?"

I nodded.

"Does this happen often?"

"What?" I asked.

He pointed to my belt. My shirt hung out ripped down the front as if torn apart in agony. My jaw ached and a trickle of water snaked down my cheek. I wiped it and saw blood.

"I'm sorry I hit you," the man said, "you rushed at my wife. Do you remember a thing?" I simply looked at my blood-smeared fingers. "Uncle? Are you okay?"

I said I was perfectly fine.

"What happened?" he persisted.

"Doggess," I said to myself.

The woman came closer pointing a cocked ear. "Doggess?" she asked in a surge of interest. The man had taken a step aside.

"Yeah," I looked her up and down, "she possesses me."

"You scared us," she shivered in respect for someone she never heard of before.

"Isn't she why you are here? She of the seven teats. What do you want from me?"

"We heard," the woman opened her mouth. Word was spreading.

"Why are you here?" I screamed.

The man came reluctantly between us. "Sacrifice," he whispered, "we want a sacrifice. What is the best time, you decide. We want the factory going next month. Is that too much to ask?"

"Yes. A life is too much to ask and a death too much to give. There are no promises to be made."

"Of course," he agreed, "when then?"

"Now," I surprised myself.

"Now? You mean now?" they spoke together.

"She's here," I spoke calmly.

"The baby?"

"Doggess, Bastards," I said and steered the guests to the rooftop. On the way, I asked Zila to follow us.

# *Chapter 23*

"Sacrifice is done at night time for two reasons," I spoke for effect. "The Gods of failure rise with the dark and the sacrificial lamb bleats the loudest, invoking them. No chants known to the mortals will suffice, but the cries of babies we can't understand. Let us not try and decipher the sounds for they are meant for the ears of the Gods. Which way east?"

They were seated on bricks placed together, and stared so hard at me to catch every word that they missed the question.

"Which way east?" I repeated. They pointed north. I placed a sheet north-south and made them sit cross-legged on it. I also ordered them to shed all inhibitions with their garments. They seemed ashamed of their bellies, and I could tell they came prepared. The man wore a starched underwear and she had weeded out all undergrowth right down to her pubes.

I placed the four bricks on a mound of white sand and seven lamps were lit around the bricks.

"She of the seven teats shall milk blood," I told no one in particular. There was a slight commotion on the stairs. Zila stood on the last step holding Kutti by the hand. And Kutti made noises meant for the Gods. The guests held hands.

"Join us," I smiled at Kutti. Pulled by the flames, she tugged at Zila's finger.

"We'll come when Kamru's here," Zila turned to go.

"Leave her here," I said quietly, "you carry on, it's alright."

The man on the sheet whispered asking if she wasn't too old.

"Let me decide what is right," said I.

The couple nodded. Kutti tottered towards the lamps like a lamb on a rock-face. I caught her arm and brought her to my lap. Zila frowned so deeply I could sense the animosity through her veil, but she took it down with her to the rest of the house. Kutti played with my chin. She chanted in a tongue of her own. I took out the only image of Nina I had, resting it against the bricks. I wound on my wrist the bloody scarf Nina last wrapped around her severed veins. Her odour still lingered, possibly in my imagination.

I told the guests, "Make love in the light of the seven flames. I must watch. "

They lay down on the hard sheet and entwined. I brought Nina's scarf to my nose and took a long whiff. Her crumpled look smiled faintly at me from the bricks. Kutti started bawling. I caught the man's eye as he relished either the chants of a toddler or the stale flesh of the woman he possessed. I cared less. *I saw Nina bathe me naked.*

I told the couple not to stop and didn't say a word to the bellowing goat on my lap. *Nina's hands were on my back. She had already taken off my shirt. She made me lie down and violently pulled off my pants.* The couple panted on the hard rough floor. The woman wrapped her legs around the man's neck. *I saw Nina walk over to the cabinet in the hall and take out a nail-cutter; she knelt down over me making clicking sounds with it. She bit my nipples with it drawing blood. I caught her hand and released it. She kept biting me on my chest, my belly, my thighs, my calves and then clicked the jaws near my ear. Mother appeared over her shoulder and grabbed her hair, pulling her away. I lunged at Mother's ankles, bringing her down. Nina held a fluttering pigeon down on her face and Mother screamed for life. A huge black tree loomed in through the window. I hacked at it with my razor. Its limbs fell off splattering blood on the walls. It howled like a thousand dogs from hell. Nina was laughing hysterically.* The woman howled and hopped in smooth slow motion on the prostrate man's loins. He sneered awkwardly. *A bitch was dragging Mother away by her neck. It turned and snarled at me. It wore my father's coat on its mangy back. I chased it far out into a field of red poppies and then ran back, scared as hell. On the bed in my room Nina sat looking at her bleeding wrists. Emarti held my razor to her throat. And slashed and slashed and slashed.*

"You bastard!" Zila cried.

I had brought the razor to the bawling goat's neck. The couple was thrashing away on the sheet. I saw Zila lunge at me and I sliced the crying with a swing of my wrist. Kutti struggled on the bricks for a litre of blood, soaked up by the sand. The couple stopped suddenly and clung to each other. I flung Zila off my back and proceeded to whip her with my belt to keep her away from tainting the sacrifice.

The man and his wife quickly collected their clothes. They bent down to be anointed in the sacrificial blood. I looked at the woman and grasped her breast and her husband looked away at Zila cowering in a corner.

"Doggess," I said, "wants you to bring me sweetened rice next Thursday. Cooked by you. And you," I turned the man's face to me, "must not repeat the mistakes of your father."

He opened his freshly bruised lips to say something, but I raised a finger. "She'll bring whatever you send with the rice, now get lost," I said.

They scurried down the stairs. I collected the sand and the sacrifice in a bag, and swung it over the parapet into the storm-drain churning the dark scum of the city towards an even murkier sea.

Zila had frozen sitting in the lotus position. I heard footsteps coming up. Kamru made an appearance in dark glasses in the dark and forced me to remove my belt once again. I could see Zila shift within her clothes as I raised the whip and rained it down on her for the next twenty minutes. Kamru just watched and I saw him return to his old domesticated self.

No one calls Uncle 'papa'.

I didn't miss Kutti much. I always thought children dangerous, enslaving almost. The younger they are, the more tenacious their control and far superior their power to influence. I think I incited the wrath of both my parents simply by being around and they invited my many happy returns by engulfing me in violence. It was Kutti's birth that turned Zila against me, and it was Kutti's death that escalated her degrees of silence. Even an unprovoked bitch will rush out of hiding to take a chunk off an unsuspecting leg just because she'd been nursing a litter. Babies inspire violence.

# Chapter 24

Word spread. Word spread amongst the influential for they were the bored lot with issues bigger than their wives. I was invited to milk them.

Kutti was long gone. Zila crinkled her stretched face at times making us believe she was smiling. Kamru fell in love with a voluminous woman of uncertain profession for a week and then sacrificed her for my sake. She met him on days he stayed out too long. Bidiya and Daya did fine on their own. Bidiya too had found a lover from her past, though he was never found after they were found out. Zila said it was a strange coincidence that the lover's disappearance and my recent short trip to Didoli had somehow overlapped, and Kamru agreed with a violent shaking of the head. Otherwise, things went on normal, until eleven half-eaten bodies of newborns washed up on the rocks, reserved for lovers, after a mighty storm one night.

To prevent matters from heating up, I asked Kamru to shut shop for a few days and told Bidiya to direct the traffic towards Daya. Daya, in turn, through her Boredom-Bedroom Project, found a very sexually inclined soul for Zila to keep her away from the house for four consecutive days. I didn't quite want her talking to strangers who came knocking. She still had no idea who Daya was and, probably, vice versa. I had forgotten to satisfy her for years and expected her to err easily at Daya's insistence. Kamru dropped her there whilst I pretended not to know anything about the entire plan.

Ready for her four day hiatus, with the mystery lover for distraction, Zila had walked up to me all dressed up and informed me she was off to Chindi. I could not read the lie on her flat face.

"But you hate the place," I toyed with her.

"I hate you too," she shut me up.

Daya called saying Zila was with a struggling artist who found her real beauty behind the expressionless mask. I felt no anger towards the boy and casually sent Kamru to give him a taste of my razor in visible portions of his body, merely to bring out the real artist in him. Kamru went a step further and brought back his middle finger.

It then occurred to me like a thunderslap - Kamru was giving vent to his own anger, not mine. The habitual whiplashes I landed on Zila's back every fortnight hurt him more than her. He was also her dog. Kamru loved Zila, I concluded, though I wasn't certain of reciprocation of such true emotions. Zila's face seldom betrayed her.

The authorities dragged up four more bodies and the newsrooms got busy. The throng at the sea-face disturbed the lovers on the rocks of whom some were, as they say, picked up for questioning. As the blind know the direction of the sun, so did the leftover lovers. They flocked to the house only to be told they had the wrong address.

On the third day, I took Kamru for a walk. He could be dying and still keep a straight face. He had given up the dark superstar glasses after the taming on the roof.

He strutted, I noticed, when I was looking away. In many ways he was like Zila. Wooden, blank, stupid, dangerous, sentimental about insignificant things and quickly forgetful when it came to emotional disasters. I made a mental note to keep them from each other for a while. Zila's absence of a few days had made him absent-minded much to my amusement. He had burnt the artist's middle-finger in a matchbox with great ceremony.

"Anything the matter?" I asked him in a serious tone, signifying stress.

"Just thinking, Boss. When I was little," he surprised me, "I wanted to be respected. Now when all these big people come to us for favours, I want something else."

"What," I enquired without revealing a smile. He rarely showed signs of not being sincere, even if it meant peeling a bucket of boiled potatoes or slicing off a digit. He walked holding his hands behind his back, deep in contemplation.

He said, "A confession." I slowed down my pace. He kept nodding his head to tell himself he had used the right word. "Yes, a confession," he said again, "from the heart."

I tried to sound okay with the idea, "What about?"

He went on rattling thoughts in his head making me get mad in mine. This was not the time for truth-telling.

He took his time and said with a deep breath, "The acid thing in Chindi."

I didn't react. The acid thing in Chindi didn't bother me that much. Zila had long ceased to be Nina.

"You know, Boss, had Zila not trusted me so, I would be okay. This is one thing on my mind constantly."

"You tell her, she'll hate you," I sounded cool.

"You don't care for her anymore, do you?" he said it like a reprimand.

"I have my ways of showing affection."

Of course, he got what I was saying. He was forever at the receiving end of my love.

We were almost at the scene of the bodies and I turned to Kamru.

"Zila's kid was yours."

"What are you saying, Boss!"

"You want to confess, you confess to me."

"What are you saying!"

"I'm saying," I gave him a hard look, "it wasn't mine. I'm sure as this razor in my coat. Was it?"

"No, Boss." I dropped the questioning. I could see some seven-eight dark-skinned men dragging a fishing net amongst the rocks with great difficulty. They kept telling each other to be careful.

"Boss," Kamru forced himself to speak, "you won't believe this."

I was listening. The razor played between my fingers.

Kamru hesitated and spoke at the same time, "It was yours."

"Even if I chop your lips off?" I said with a short laugh.

"Even then, Boss. You were not yourself when this happened. You were definitely not you."

"What was I, the seven-teat-bitch?" I peered into his face in mock-belief.

"I don't know, Boss, you were," he stopped.

"Yeah?"

"You were like a mad dog, Boss. I could not pull you off."

"Yeah? You were there? Doing what?"

"I heard her cries and came. You were throwing her across the room," he didn't want to go on. I put a hand on his shoulder. "The kid was yours, Boss. I'm as sure as the knife in your pocket. Whoever

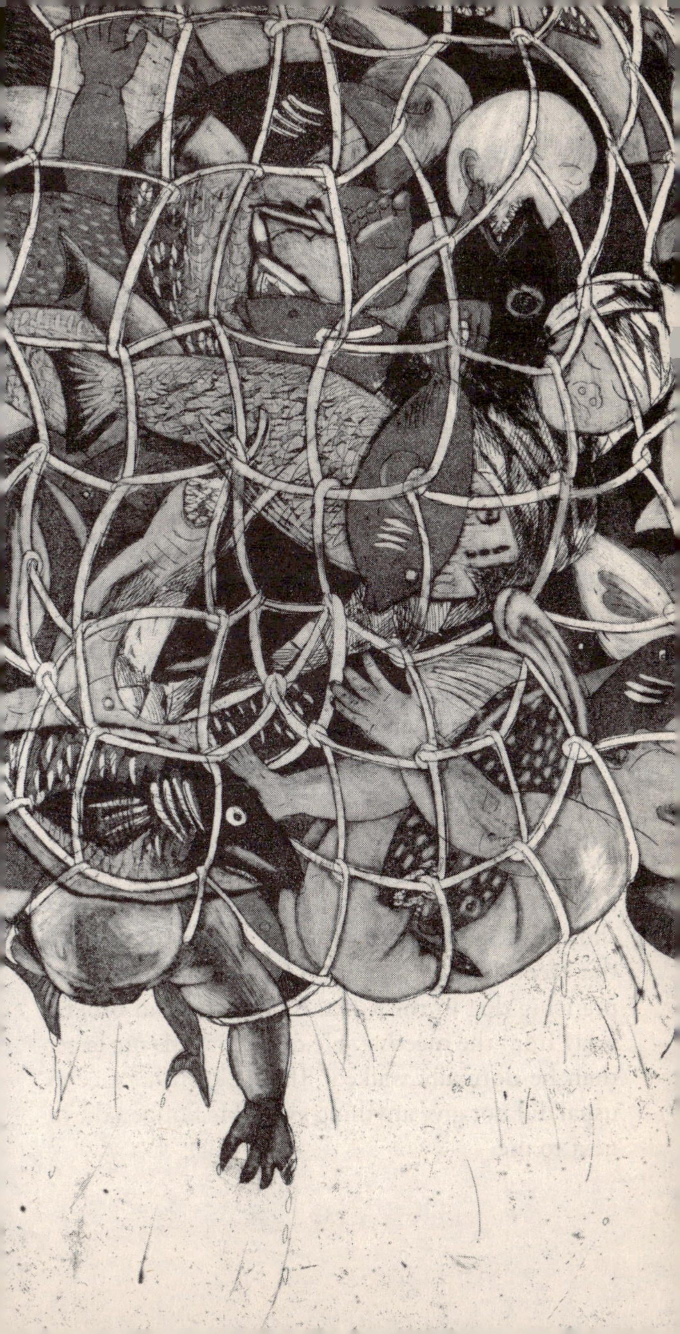

you were, you were on her."

I walked on silently, not fully comprehending Kamru's news. It seemed Zila's convenient pregnancy might not have been so convenient for her after all. I tried to remember the incident, but nothing came to mind. I was nearing seventy. Seriously, my life was acting funny.

One of the fishermen waved to the officials at the edge. "Two more in the net," he shouted.

"Makes it twenty-one," said one, and the others shook their heads in disapproval. I gestured to Kamru to go and see what the fuss was. I waited under the sun. My head had a weight tied above the right ear. Kamru was leaning right over the heads of people awaiting the haul and cast glances in my direction to see if I was alright. A bloated urchin revolved around me mumbling for money as he rubbed his tummy. I took out my blade and showed him how sharp it was, which made him retreat to a woman walking her dog. She too saw the group discussing in a huddle and went over to check if she was missing something important. I heard a short shriek. The curious lady rushed away from the scene holding her heart in one hand and the prancing dog in the other. Kamru too had broken away from the meeting. He came towards me faster than he normally walked. The look on his face as usual did not give anything away. He flopped down next to me.

"You okay, Boss?"

I said if I wasn't I would tell him and that he should stick to the story we were after.

"This is something else," he talked in riddles.

"Come to the point," I was losing patience, "I've had enough of you today. Get on with it."

"These bodies aren't ours."

"Not? Twenty-one babies and not one of them is ours?"

"No, Boss. These two have parts missing."

"The fish got them," I snapped.

"No, Boss, no animal. Someone cut them out. They said so."

"Let's get back," I could feel a fever coming on. My over-sensitive ears were burning.

"We have competition," Kamru voiced my concern grimly.

# Chapter 25

I had two theories: either this person was a hunter or a scavenger. Either he cut up his own goats or fished out ours from the storm drain, cut out parts and tossed them back. Either way wasn't good for our reputation. We decided to keep vigil.

The nights were warm and Zila's extended absence made them tolerable. I decided to sleep on the rooftop until she came back. Things fell into place beautifully with no guests, no Zila, no shrill bells and all the time to watch out for the scavenger if there was one. If Kamru's story was true, I thought, I could very well be the one. I was laughing at my little joke when Kamru came up the stairs with food and liquor, both not for me.

"You really won't eat?" he asked me. I wiped my eyes. He looked surprised. "You laughing or crying?"

"What's the difference, my faithful dog," I laughed at him, "between love and hate? Aren't they one and the same?"

"I'm not a man of such depth," he said sourly.

"Deep down we are all bastards. There is no point going deep down. You can see everything from up here."

"Sometimes it is impossible to understand you, Boss," he poured himself a drink and offered it to me.

"Did you do it?" I asked point-blank.

"I told you it was you," he wore a pained look. "Now don't kill my peg."

"I'm asking about the bodies. It was you, right? You cut out their hearts."

Kamru took a sip and stopped. He threw the brass thing he was drinking from, and some of his cheap liquor splashed my toe. I didn't mind a little show of emotion here and there, if it was genuine. The dog would deny and deny and deny, until he broke down and blurted out everything. Next, he would fall on my wet feet, begging to be spared the blade. I prepared myself for the act of forgiveness. But Kamru remained silently shaking his leg.

I picked up his cup from the farthest corner of the roof and refilled it. He did not accept it to give weight to his sulk. I heard a sound. Throwing down the cup, I rushed back to the edge and looked down.

"Kamru," I called out to the scowler, "come here you pisspot." He dragged himself up reluctantly to the parapet. "What do you see down there?"

He looked as if he was doing me a favour and then drawled sourly, "Two people. Twins."

"Where's the second?" I could see just one man with long hair, wallowing in the drain. He had in his hand a box or something even my father couldn't make out from up there. By the way he moved, like a blind man feeling the city's excreta with his outstretched hands, he was definitely searching for something useful, dead babies perhaps.

"I can only see double at night when I don't have my drink, Boss." So I made him drink from the bottle and fell down laughing at the most seriously told joke in the world. "I mean it," Kamru said flatly.

"I know," I wiped my tears for the second time, "now look down and tell me what you see." He tried to take another swig and I caught his throat with a threat, "When I say see, you see. Don't make me speak double."

He was back to himself soon enough. He wanted to go down and take a look. I waited for his return. The man in the drain stood chest-deep in the muck feeling about for fresh bodies, I was more than sure. I noticed something else too: the man was a woman. A slight change in my breathing told me I must follow my dog down the stairs.

On the fourth step below the first landing I found a woman's blouse, which had no business being there. I saw Kamru putting on his rubber slippers in case he had to enter the drain. He was, I could tell, watching me pick up the blue blouse with tiny mirror-work. He caught my eye and glanced away. *The pain above my ear began to throb silently. I thought I smelled a fragrance of clove and jasmine beaten together in a brass mortar.* Kamru came up to me to ask if I was coming too. I told him to get out of my sight and get into the ditch or bitch. *An anger rose in my groin. One of the doors squeaked open. Anisa ran out of Room 8, naked, squealing as a pig. Who opened the door?* I yelled for Kamru. Then I remembered he was chasing the woman in the drain outside. *I knew this girl's name was Anisa, somehow. She sat astride on the railing swinging her legs. I held out her blouse to her. My head was taking a load of a wet cement bag dropped from a height.*

*"Put it on," she said.*

*"I have a headache," I snorted.*

*"Put it on then," she smiled, "it'll take the pain away."*

*I came towards her and tried to put her arm through the sleeve. She pushed me away screaming, "Not me, Bastard, you put it on. Dare you touch me again I'll chop your claws."*

*I felt four hands grab my legs and four hands grab my arms. They dropped me on my back on the stairs and I saw their faces. I knew their names but they didn't occur to me then. Five boys in the same blue uniform as mine, had me pinned to the marble. The same boys from my childhood. They shouted obscenities and hurled punches at my face and gut.*

*"Make him put it on," hopped Anisa on one leg, clapping her hands. They tore off my clothes, tied the blouse to my chest and began dancing and yelling around me. My head imploded. I saw Anisa run back into her room. The boys slid down the railing one by one, whooping like cranes. I lay there pulling my hair, fighting back blood in my eyes.* Kamru had vanished. I tried calling out for him and no words escaped me. My back hurt from the fall.

*"You go back and beat them," I heard Mother say. I couldn't move a nerve. She kicked me on the calves again, and again, and again. I told her to get lost, to leave me alone, that she was hurting me. She said she wanted a son who could stand up to his bullies at school. A son, not a eunuch. I pushed her away and stumbled blindly down.*

*"Wait till you get home," she screamed, "I'll teach you to steal the maid's blouses. I'll teach you to go into Anisa's room. You just come back and watch what I do."*

I ran away from the voices and out of the house. The cool air almost killed me with relief. I kept running looking over my shoulder. I couldn't decipher what was happening. I expected Anisa, the maid, to race after me with her blouse; I looked around for the bullies as I ran ahead, wide-eyed and panting. I banged into someone who held me firmly by the arms. Everything went out of focus.

"What happened, Boss?" I heard Kamru

whisper. I saw him grinning into my face. "I'm glad you came."

The night sky was clear as hell. There was a stench of familiar make in the air. We stood at the edge of the storm-drain, all empty of the woman I saw from up there.

"I found no one," Kamru complained, "maybe he drowned."

My nerves reverberated. I slapped him.

Back in the house, because Kamru was extra chatty, I concluded he was hiding an anaconda under his, whatever little, thinning hair. A man who has just been slapped tells the slapper stories of him bathing in the stream of his childhood, only if he has committed murder a while ago. I watched every word, every twitch adorning his lips, waiting for a slip and fall. I had solid intuition to believe there lived a direct connection between the blouse, the woman, her disappearance and the crap coming out of Kamru's trap.

"Boss, four of them drowned," he was saying, "with their bicycles. We found them miles downstream. One happened to be a cousin in his fifteenth year. I never touched the river ever. A vulture had his head inside the boy's gut. Looked funny, you know, like a headless bird flapping its wings. I once caught a snake with a frog in its throat. It can't do a thing until the frog gets swallowed completely. It looked real crazy croaking. A croaking snake. I put my foot on its tail and let it dance. You know, Boss, what happened next?" I had never seen Kamru so talkative, not even when he came back from Chindi. The woman was not in the drain, she was in the house. I was so sure, I caught the dog by his loose collar and put the razor to his ear.

"I don't want stories, my friend," I smiled, "tell me the truth and I'll forgive you. You keep silent, and I have your ear one slice at a time. Tell me the story of the woman in the drain."

"You said man," he swallowed, "I came looking for a man."

"I changed my mind," I tapped his temple with the blunt edge. He was about to give way I could see. Kamru didn't waste too much time defending a lie.

"Who was she?" I nudged the confession over the edge.

"Nobody you know, Boss," he had learnt to craft his words.

"I'm sure," I exclaimed, "can you tell her to come out?"

Kamru grinned in a sheepish shameless way, "She's in the Vulture Room, Boss. Now can you put it down?" The bastard had calculated I would never look there with Emarti's garlanded picture staring at me. Even in death she gave me the bouts. She conjured up images of Nina's bleeding wrists and never of her own sliced neck.

For Kamru's part in the evening adventure, I took his hairy earlobe with a clean swipe of the razor. He howled and clutched his ear, but uttered not a word of protest in acceptance of his betrayal. I forgave him quickly and strode into Emarti's lair, wiping the blade on the blouse that had attached itself to my shirt by a hook in the back. I meant to ask Kamru, when he recovered, what the blouse on the stairs meant. Meanwhile, I sneezed ten times in a row. The allergy was nowhere near gone.

Emarti smiled benignly. I smeared the blood from my finger on her glass face. The grainy picture looked so reverential, it gave me an idea I decided to keep for another day.

"I'll tell you all you want to know," a voice came through the bathroom door, "but promise me you'll turn your back and let me walk away." *I felt a fire burn on my neck.*

"I do the dictating around here," I said.

She didn't play any more games and came directly, "I saw that a moment ago."

"I'm good with that sort of thing. Now step out and kill my curiosity." My neck was biting me like Kamru's ear just then. My aches and pains were getting more frequent, I noted.

"Okay, I'm coming out. Just put the thing away."

I closed the razor on my chest. The bathroom

door creaked open. Kamru was right I did not know this person. I'd never seen her before. She came right at me and stood swinging side-to-side, unafraid. The stink of the drain, though quickly washed, still emanated from the pores of her skin and the coarse white cottons clinging to her.

"Happy?" she said, "Now you can watch me as much as you want. Have your fill."

I eased myself down on the bed and let her swing her stuff in front of me. She looked, I guessed, around fifty-eight and had probably never borne children. Her hips were slim and her structure not too bony. She dyed her hair not completely, just around the top of her head. Her eyes were two kohl holes shining in their depths a kind of discomforting brilliance that could drill a tunnel through the night. Her bangles clinked as did all the silver all over her. She wasn't beautiful or anything, but the sandalwood paste on her forehead gave her the dignity I did not respect.

"May I go now?" she shifted on her feet. The swaying of the hips had stopped. A frown had obscured the sandalwood. And she looked away from where I sat in the manner of a girl hiding a minor mischief. Her voice had a familiarity I could not place. *The pinching sensation on my neck was behaving like a stab.* These sudden discomforts were really happening too often, too randomly.

"Have you finished or you want me to dance

for you?" *The voice troubled me now.*

"Why do you steal my bodies? What does Kamru get out of this? Tell me."

She started to laugh. I wore my weary look and she shut up. I repeated the question by raising my brow. If I were to go deeper into her laughter, I was certain I'd discover a nervousness that would tell me a lot more than I wanted to know.

"Two questions," she ruminated. I nodded a bored head on a painful neck. "Kamru gets pleasure and I take the hearts. Now happy?"

"Why take the hearts?" I already had a clue, still I asked.

"You throw away the bodies, I take them. How does it matter why or what?" she grew bolder.

I leaned forward and took hold of her right hand, "Why take the hearts?" I had her middle finger in my fist. Her eyes panicked and beads appeared above her lips. I flipped open the razor smoothly.

She said, "I sell them. Burn them. Sacrifice them for diseases of death. A baby's heart is difficult. A drowned heart works better than a cremated one." The blade was talking. "Kamru tells me when to come and I just remove the heart and go. No harm meant. Today, I came on my own and found nothing."

"Who believes this?" I asked merely to make conversation and not get an answer.

"You do," she smiled, "I do. So many not ready for death would die for a baby's heart to save them. They would do anything I told them to do with it. You know the business."

I let go her finger and she held it in her other hand close to the heart like something precious she'd lost and found. I came to the conclusion, "I want my share. You take the hearts by all means, still I want my share."

"Sounds good," she said quickly, "How much, Uncle?"

"All," I answered. She seemed confused. I just nodded my head to an imaginary tune.

She said she was fine as long as she got her raw material for free. But when I told her she worked for me now and would get wages, she again said fine though many shades lighter. I told her to go away instantly and thanked her for the impending collaboration. When she reluctantly held out her hand to mine to seal the deal, I sacrificed half her middle finger in the same friendly way I had taken Kamru's ear. She made no noise. Just put her hand in her mouth and walked out delirious like a drunk.

I never told anyone I knew who she was. I know where that voice came from. Why my neck pain disappeared the moment she left the room, I had figured out.

This was the keeper of the temple of the altar. She was the voice who bit the lump off my neck after the hospital disrespected me. And now she was my bitch licking her wound. She took my tumour, I took her finger. She took my hearts, I took her art. She played Kamru, I play my usual ping pong.

# *Chapter 26*

We diversified again, though managers may call it the evolution of an existing business. But before we launched into the new story, a slight skirmish left an after-vomit taste. Actually, the police came enquiring, in time for breakfast, a few days after Chanana went home sans a finger. Her name was Chanana and I suspected she was angry at her loss and bitterly vengeful, almost enough to castrate our success. It would have been considered foolish, and highly suicidal, of her to tip-off the law.

The knock on the door had a tone different from the ones we usually opened the rooms to. Kamru and I glanced at each other. His appearance had become a lot more interesting minus the earlobe. I motioned for him to invite trouble inside.

A boyish man in a t-shirt and shorts asked Kamru if he was aware of the dead babies in the sea. Kamru didn't know what the chap was talking about, so I got up to save the situation in case he began overacting his ignorance.

"We even saw some," I said, "very badly chewed."

"By crocodiles," Kamru added.

And I gently corrected him, "Fish, Idiot. You don't find crocodiles in the sea." Then turning to our guest I uttered a sentence out of some grandmotherly movie, "Are you the new neighbour down the road?"

He didn't answer. He should have been in the periphery of twenty-eight and his clothes betrayed his age by a thousand years. He crossed the door acting as though it was his dad's property, but I merely measured his neck with my eyes. I followed him up the stairs.

"How many people live here?" he asked at last, pushing open rooms randomly.

"As many as you see."

"I want direct answers, Uncle. I'm on deputation. Think and answer. How many people?"

"Two of us and quite a few ghosts." I completely forgot Zila.

"You and the duffer? What took his ear?"

"Crocodile," I said. He surveyed the Vulture Room.

"Please take your shoes off," I told him a trifle sternly, "this is religion."

He stayed at the door and his gaze strayed to where Emarti sat staring like divinity. He even bowed his head a bit, and I grinned at what all absurd powers ambiguity possessed. The man had turned into a nodding piece of mud - if mud could nod. I told him he should ask for a wish and it would be granted, soon enough.

"I want the butchers," he blinked at me.

"Then you shall have them," I said.

"I feel I have them already."

"I hope you don't mean us," I was enjoying this.

He seemed taken aback by the innocence in my enquiry and stopped talking. I led him up the stairs to the roof from where he dropped a brick into the storm-drain below, after carefully measuring the air with his eyes. He appeared satisfied and to please him further, I too threw a bottle into the quietly flowing muck.

"I can do that too," I joked. He didn't utter a squeak and we came down to where Kamru was finishing his milk at the table. We pulled out chairs.

"What's the odour?" the man sniffed awkwardly. I pointed at Kamru. And Kamru buried his face in the glass, insulted. I poured tea for three and that reminded me of Zila.

"My wife is out," I played the perfect citizen, "if it means anything to the investigation. She's back in two days. The officer thinks we've been killing babies and chucking them in the drain," I told Kamru. Kamru tilted his head towards our guest with the most cherubic face I'd seen. He could have been listening to a devotional song on morning radio.

"I'll take your friend to the station for a while," the man extracted my permission. I said that was absolutely fine if, he could be back in time for the evening prayer at six.

"You wouldn't want my wife in for questioning?" I called out after them. I didn't get an answer. Kamru returned at five in reply. He had been beaten in ways that displayed no bruises. I felt bad. Two days later, I was told the officer was shipped out of the city. We had a list of regular visitors with some clout, and they did not want us inconvenienced in any way. After a week, our man was found miscarried on a train, missing a finger.

We opened the doors of the Vulture Room to devotees.

We had graduated to a state of bliss. Bidiya, Daya, Chanana, Zila, Kamru and I. A slight shuffle in the roles made things easier, even though not one of them knew exactly how many were there in the loop, not even Kamru.

Bidiya started sourcing babies from Didoli, while she continued to send college-going girls to Daya in the night shift. Daya's Boredom-Bedroom division was also going packed and she did complain of too less time for herself. We moved the sacrifices to Chanana's temple of the altar so that she didn't have to travel all the way for the hearts. She was glad she had been taken over with a steady chain of clients and raw material. Zila handled the traffic at the house together with an equally uninspired Kamru. And I devoted my energy to Emarti's devotees, who had become a rising stream of domestic frustrations. Eventually, I planned to move the rest of the business out of the house. The integration of blood, desire and belief was becoming a working reality.

Emarti in death was more likeable than an eating-burping-farting Emarti. The bed and all other peripherals had been taken away from around her image, smothered in marigold, and replaced by wall-to-wall mattresses covered in white sheets sourced from the same chap who supplied to the local hospitals of repute. The Vulture Room wore serenity, I wore silence in abundance. Zila had fashioned a garment for me out of used jute bags discarded by a tobacco wholesaler and, I must admit, it commanded a lot of interest and respect in certain circles. Kamru and she remained invisible in plain whites.

Emarti's reputation wasn't just spreading, it was spawning and my dearest desire became to put Zila's picture beside hers before the year expired. I rarely gave much thought to the finances making their way in, for it was the pleasure of the endeavour that drove me still. About Kamru and Zila, I was a little sceptical when I found them talking so often with pursed lips in my presence. I also noticed an odd coincidence: they always whistled a particular tune before they had something to say to me. Like the phone rings before you take a call, they whistled first and then addressed me. No, it wasn't as if they were calling a dog, it was more like background music in an average movie. I had heard the melody somewhere and each time it played, it made me temporarily mellow like warm yellow honey.

Coming to the business of blessing the unfortunate, I had nothing much to offer except a long session of complete silence. The devotees - all women - sat on the floor and kept their mouths shut. After thirty days of abstinence from any utterance between nine and five, a follower was allowed to enter my chamber, the erstwhile bathroom from which Chanana had emerged from hiding.

I asked the believer if she was happy which, of course, no woman ever is. And when she finished telling her stale tale of demons and bastards, I asked her if she really wanted a solution or secretly enjoyed her torture.

"I want freedom," was the normal cry of confusion.

"I don't think so," I would say and ask her to leave.

"But I came here for an answer," she pleads.

I say, "You are the problem. Go solve yourself first, is what SHE wants of you. You have not the courage to confront your own demons. SHE wants you to go."

"What must I do?" she folds her hands. I know this is the sign and put her to the test.

"You are not ready yet to conquer yourself."

"I have not waited for a month to be asked to go away. Please tell me what I must do."

"You are ashamed of yourself. Come back when you are not."

"I'm here to learn, to find the way. Please show me the way. Teach me to be free of myself."

"Take your clothes off," I tell her and wait for the shockwaves to settle. She obviously hesitates and even looks over her shoulders suspiciously. "See, you are ashamed of yourself!" I tell her with a laugh that could mean 'I was just testing you' or 'I was damn serious' or both. In ninety-five percent of the cases, as in a cheap film, she wants to stay and see what happens. She has already crossed the line and she'll wait for anything to turn her world around. The five percent who scare themselves away would come back some day when an inevitable disaster strikes in a fragile moment. The best part is that women can and cannot keep a secret best from the rest of the world.

"SHE wants that you take your clothes off," I tell the ninety-five percent and they shed all inhibitions in an instant, as if a switch has been thrown.

"Go look at yourself in the mirror," I point to the corner behind the newbie, "and light the candle on the ledge to the right. SHE wants to know what you see."

She kindles the candle in five or six shaky strikes, her lips quiver as she steals a glance at her familiar faults. She covers the parts of her body she consider ungainly and, drops the hand by her side if she sees me watching her.

"Do you notice the knots in your body? They are the knots in your mind. You are not ashamed of your body, it's your mind your body wants to change. See the glass of milk over there?"

She nods slowly. Her whole system is already comfortable in my divine presence, and her own. I ask her to drink it if she can. She picks it up and takes a short sip. It's bitter so she makes a face.

"It's not milk," I warn her, "it will make you forget. Memory is a bitch. It dogs you." Women are suckers for this kind of vague nonsense full of metaphors.

"I wish to forget a lot," says she predictably.

"SHE says you drink it and die for the day to be reborn by the night," I try not to sound funny, just the right dose of casual and serious theatre. The woman finishes the drink in one gulp to impress HER. I open a door at the back leading to the staircase leading to a room and lock her in for a couple of hours. No one sees her go. The rest of the women sit silently in the Vulture Room awaiting the day of their deliverance.

The sleeping woman wakes up to find her covered by a silk sheet and, as she soon discovers, completely untainted. Her head is a bit heavy, but her spirit is willing to trust. Before she knocks, I open the door in my rags and hand her over the clothes she shed.

"Are you better?" I enquire.

She bursts into tears.

"Are you ashamed of what you just did?"

She shakes her head slowly after a minute of reflection.

"Then let us meet again after a month and cure the spirit, that lying bastard child within us all." She wants to know how she could repay me. "Pay HER when you believe you are HER," I see her off philosophically.

The dessert is: not once does she call me 'Uncle'.

Twenty-two percent of the women go to the next level. These are the hardcore desperate cases, having no solid reason to be wretched. Their problem is they have no real problem other than themselves. They take off from where they left thirty days ago, ready to experiment. A rich lawyer's second wife was one of the first at my disposal.

"Bound by the past?" I met her in Room 6 and smiled kindly.

"Past or present, I don't know," she folded her arms across her naked chest. "Why is a man so needed?"

When a blind person recognizes your voice,

he wants to believe you while walking on fire. The woman sat unclothed on a bed and the fact that she was willing to tell her deepest aches in a darkened room meant she was ready to cross all hurdles placed by her upbringing. I told her a little secret.

"A woman is a woman's biggest enemy. Who is yours?"

"So many," she said instantly.

"No, there is always only one. Who is yours?"

"My husband travels a lot and," she was going to narrate a stupid story of betrayal and I told her she was wrong.

"My own mother?"

"No, wrong again."

We sat silently for a very long ticking of the clock until she saw the enemy within. Her guilt-ridden eyes rose and fell when I shifted on the chair in my jute bag suit. The evening session of silence in the Vulture Room was over and I heard the devotees shuffling down to the main door. I had all the time since the evening traffic too had moved to Daya.

"Did you sleep better this month?" I asked and then continued, "You didn't is why we are here."

"I wasn't ashamed of myself anymore," she spoke a little louder to demonstrate her confidence.

"Still you are here. You asked why a man is needed."

She nodded.

"A man isn't needed," I smiled as a father, "we fool ourselves into believing that he is. Isn't it true?"

She nodded again, a little uncertainly. I waited for a more emphatic answer. After pretending to think deeply she said, "Yes."

I came abruptly, "Pleasure yourself."

"Hmmm?"

"Believe you are free."

"I am free."

"But you are here. You are listening to me. I am the same old material your husband is made of. How are you free?" My self-deprecating honesty was beginning to play tricks. She needed a gentler push, this clod of mud.

She nodded in understanding. I pushed a bottle of liquor across the bed. "You are staying the night. Finish this. SHE wants you to believe you are free. Some good shall come out of it." And I left the room, locking it behind me. She threw up in the night and went away in the morning. All for free.

A month later she slept with a stranger in the same room. All for free.

Soon after, she sacrificed a goat at the rooftop. All for free.

She wore an image of HER around her neck. Her troubles quadrupled because she still held on to her past. Give yourself up completely, I told her on her way to Chanana's.

She sacrificed her own blood from a gash on

her palm at the altar. All for free.

"Are you happier now," I asked her.

She nodded.

"Sacrifice is the road to happiness," I explained, "this is what you came looking for. This is what you must do to kill sorrow. Pain is pleasure, sorrow isn't. Now you are free. Now SHE is happy. Now you are HER." All for free.

She nodded. And kept coming back for more freedom. I remember counting twenty seven cuts on her.

One day I said to her, "I met a man who wants to do business with another man. A huge deal worth millions."

She looked confused, "What stops him then?" I think she was waiting for a lesson in this, latching on to every word I was about to utter. I took her for a walk around a dying tree.

"There's a problem," I continued in the same vein, of telling a parable.

She knitted her brow and appeared learned, "Aren't problems the solutions themselves?"

"Of course. The problem is a third man."

"Then he is also the solution."

"Exactly," I exclaimed, pretending she had surprised me with her intellect.

"Is this a true story?" she beamed at the applause in her head. And when I said it was, which indeed was correct, she announced excitedly, "Then the third man should help the other two close the deal."

I waited for thirty meaningful seconds before letting her into it, "You are the third person."

She gaped and gasped and looked at my solemnity and asked, "Me? I'm nobody."

"You are the wife of the man who won't let this transaction through. It is the second businessman's lawyer who is the problem. Only you can convince him otherwise," I smiled. "SHE wants you to. Will you?"

She nodded her signature nod.

The deal came through. My new business made a killing. All for free.

As usual, word went around that I controlled the better half of influence and affluence. To the business of desire, blood and belief I added a fourth dimension: power.

Wealth was always a given.

# *Chapter 27*

I realized I was spending a lot of time with Daya whenever I had gypsy minutes. As a rule, I never went to the house she ran nor enquired of the number of cabs that ran her Boredom-Bedroom Project; we exchanged currency and incidents in nondescript eateries in the suburbs where our businesses had no business to be.

"Don't trust your flat-faced woman," she once mentioned.

"You don't trust Zila or you telling me not to trust her?" I always put her in her place if she ever played the ambition game with me. That closed her mouth till she had to put food in it. "Why did you say such a thing?" I asked her randomly when we met next. She smiled like she was waiting for me to come down to earth. I liked the way she never wagged her tail. The other thing I found beautiful was that she killed her man and enjoyed it as a cow chewing cud, no regrets.

"I get the feeling she is using that man."

"Kamru?" I said it like it was decayed news.

"I see them together a lot."

I raised a 'where' with my eyes. I wasn't bothered or anything, just curious. Daya took her time to answer. I got the feeling she was suppressing a laugh.

"I saw them at the house," she said, "in one of the rooms."

"You were at the house?" my anger rose. "You are not supposed to be there, Bitch."

She had the gall to play with me, I liked that too. But her enthusiasm had to be managed. I put the razor on the table. She started smirking. She placed a hand on my hand and said with a flash in her eyes, "They were at my house, you crumbling piece of architecture. They were in a room at my house."

Passion took time to settle down before the absurdity of the rendezvous sank in. Zila and Kamru had found a love-nest on my mango tree. An earless man deserved a faceless woman. They were victims of a concept they had helped propagate. I cracked up at the irony of those two looking for a room. Daya too smiled, then giggled and then laughed till moisture appeared on her eye-ends. A couple of wasters at the next table grinned for nothing.

"You saw them?" The thought of putting Zila in a picture frame beside Emarti recurred as strongly as the suspicion of Daya using this information to gain favour. I was terribly amused by the whole scenario. I had sent Zila to her not so long ago. Kamru had dropped her there and only went later to collect the artist-boyfriend's finger. He had managed getting his own finger in the pie, I guffawed. But, I had recently heard of another close collaboration that bothered me more than this. It was about time I revealed the nugget.

"What's so funny," Daya dabbed an eye.

"Bidiya hasn't come down for a while," I changed the subject, "any idea why?" I could see slight discomfort curl up my advisor's little finger. She tried clearing a cavity with her tongue. I waited for an answer.

"How does it matter as long as we are getting our girls," she said this in a way Nina would call 'evasive'. Nina had her own strategies for arriving at the truth and for Nina, avoiding a direct question was alarming. I, on the contrary, never lost sleep over sudden suspicions because trust was just an enamelled iron mug that had to rust some day.

"How many husbands did you say you killed?" I asked her.

She remained silent, but looked at me point-blank. I toyed with the razor, spinning it around. The waiter came and went. I heard a bone crack in my knee.

She said, "Bidiya is here. In the house. My house."

"Oh!" I tried to sound surprised.

"She recognised Zila and the scum."

"I know. I sent them there," I lied to seem in control and added in a whisper, "but Bidiya I did not send to you. You forgot to tell me of your growing sisterhood."

She was taken aback, though appeared calm. "What will you do, kill me for withholding nothing?" she provoked me.

"You didn't tell me how many husbands you killed?" I like my questions to be fed.

"Just one rat."

I gave her the razor. "Here, take it. I'm putting my finger on the table, I want you to cut it off. I won't make a sound." My gaze sat steadily on her as she swallowed the implications of my offer.

"You like drama," her upturned lip hissed finally, "what if I take the whole hand?"

"Do it."

She threw up her hands, "You're making a mess of it, Uncle. I warned you about your bitch and you're taking it personally." I knew my proposition had shocked her into submission once more but, I just hoped she knew what she was saying.

"I am okay if you kill five more husbands," I said, "but no politics. Tell Bidiya, without telling her, to stay in Didoli. Keep your woman locked inside you. I'm not here to hear gossip, Bitch, I want blood."

"I get it now," she cast a meaningful glance at me.

"That saves me a finger," I got up.

"You didn't like me knowing this baby business, no? You don't want your puppets getting entangled, Uncle. Is that what this is? Daya knows Bidiya knows Kamru knows Zila knows who else? Have I got it all? You know very well who out of this riff-raff can run the show after you, and so do I. You have been out here having tea with me so often, why? You want to know what I know. I am your successor and you know it," she stated matter-of-factly.

Logic is a fool, intuition never fails. My greatest nightmare was sitting across the table narrating her weakness: she was exactly my blood group and I could read her mind days before she had a thought worth worrying about. She was telling me what I had been telling myself, and it was good that things were out in the open in my territory. It was true Daya knew more than she should have. But at the end of the day, she had killed only one husband and all the board members, other than her, were well aware of my capabilities with the razor. For a while longer, I let her believe in her skills.

Till she was silent, Daya was a serpent. Now, she was a mere pup barking up the wrong Uncle.

Seven Sundays later, we met up at a lunch table. By her costume it was evident she was on her way to a wedding. Her eyes had turned green, her lips painted mould-blue and her hair added a good four inches to her self-consciousness. She slipped into a chair across me as a bride at a mass marriage.

"What's the occasion," I broke the glass wall.

She looked at me differently today and her voice had a flute-like quality, "You've stopped coming over and I don't like it. Just because we had a little argument, does that mean we are not lovers anymore?"

She gushed. I glanced up from the fork I was balancing on a jug and met her eyes midway in the air like sparklers. Her breathing came in bursts of a runner trying to not appear out of breath. She, hiding her anxiety, made me edgy and so I let the statement pass. What news was she about to puke, I wondered, to get back on top in the power pyramid? My hunch pointed to some disparaging remark downsizing Bidiya in the hope of erasing all doubts of conspiracy.

Daya placed her lacquered yellow bag on the table and, unbecoming of her, withdrew from its gut a red lipstick and proceeded to run it over her frosty lips before I could warn her. The original blue lips shone through on the edges giving the impression she was happily suffocating. For some reason this brought to mind Emarti, instantly killing my appetite. I told the hovering waiter to go away for a while to let me think. Daya devoured me with her affectations of affection.

"You have been following me around," she giggled, "and now you are going all bashful. It's charming to see such innocence in these times." I waited for her to strike the nail and she, being an old hand, was pottering around listening for cracks in my silence. A snake is a snake until it has decayed to good-quality manure, for even the bones of a dead snake are known to cause serious harm.

"Bidiya runs a house in Didoli", she squealed, "Only white men. Kamru tells her when you are coming and she covers up. Are you listening?"

"Tell me something new," said I plainly.

"You know what?" she said after a while, having made no strong impression upon me.

I really had no way of reading her mind, so I made a funny face that usually means 'get on with it'. I also called the waiter over.

She placed a hand on my hand by a habit recently acquired and told me, "You offered me your finger the last time. Well I want it now." Her tone was bold, challenging. This was exactly how a respectable rich whore whose advances had been spurned was expected to behave.

"Today the offer has escalated," I was happier at her return of form. From my trousers I threw the razor at her. It bounced off the jug and landed crookedly on her empty plate with a double clang. "You get to slice my throat in front of these utterly pretentious people or, if you want, privately at a more worthy location. I'm serious."

She held the instrument pensively to gauge my reaction after all the bravado steeped in elegant words. I watched her knock the metallic blunt edge of the blade on the porcelain plate, in wonderment. At her transformation from a schoolgirl in pigtails moments ago to a silent unpredictable woman of cold intentions. Had I not had anything to lose, I would have frowned concern for my safety. I tread on her sores instead.

"I did not ask you to play with it," I said scratching an invisible stain on my nose. "Give it back to me if you've lost your bite and let me show you how not to sacrifice your luck."

She stared at me for a stony minute and slid the razor across the table. The waiter waited patiently listening to our game of ping-pong. I whispered to him and he said 'pardon', so I told him to bend closer. His ear was five inches from my mouth when I whipped out Mason's old razor and placed the blade on his throat. He started heh-hehing stupidly and I cut his laughter into two.

He sat down on the extra chair, spurting red paint across his ironed shirt. Daya sat with her hand to her mouth. The only other couple, at the far end, was busy with some meat too tough to handle. The sloppy manager took orders on the phone in a nasal irritating voice. I got up and walked out of Heats

Up Eats in a brisk shuffle followed by Daya at a trot, just two steps behind. We turned an abrupt corner into a brimming paper market encouraging us to get lost. If not a soul in the street noticed blood on my shirt, I would not be surprised at the blindness of our times; and if someone did, I cared not under the happy circumstances. Daya had been tamed satisfactorily for the time being - and I never look back when I have a bus called business to catch. Thirty-eight minutes later, Daya stammered, "What if he survives?"

I loved her optimism so much I gave her another chance.

# Chapter 28

Much after marrying us at the cremation ground, Ari made an appearance at the house with a simple enough request - the eunuch community was meeting up in the city and needed the house for outstation delegates for a week - which I promptly refused. Ari got up with a weak 'okay' as if I owed it to her and I told her not to take this as the end of our acquaintance.

She sat down again smelling of day-old sweat. "I like your honesty, Uncle, but we must help each other. Kamru sounded fine the other day, so I came."

Kamru nodded from his end.

"He has the brain of an elephant," I said, "He thinks the man sitting on his head is poking him out of love. He doesn't understand business and I don't understand favours."

"You have your ways," Ari laughed casting a glance at Kamru as a sign of no love lost between them. I merely smiled. We sat around drinking

Kamru's cheap liquor in Room 3 because it was slightly removed from the rest of the house and our words, which I suspected could be of a sensitive nature, would not be carried out. We had pulled two chairs close to a low table and I sat on the bed making my position clear. I did feel a trifle ashamed of being in the room with them, and their sitting so close made me angry. I could see a pair of cracked heels and painted toes almost touching the bottle on the table.

"You can't live alone on an island, Uncle," Ari was saying, "unless you are the island."

"I am the island," I said dryly. I wanted them to go and die that very instant, in front of my smarting eyes.

She laughed showing off her bad teeth, "Say, Uncle, is there no way to bribe your stubborn head because, like they all say, you lost your cold heart in the snow and turned it to ice." I listened to her metaphors dipped in bile and took a long burning sip in an attempt to hide my grin. "Don't mind what I blurt out now for it is the liquor talking, but one thing every bugger in the city believes is how even the vultures won't mess with you when you are found dead in a ditch."

I saw Kamru smirking behind a thoughtful fist covering his lips. He caught my glare and cleared his throat. "You are very quiet," I donated to the sarcasm in the air.

"Just listening, Boss, there is nothing I can add."

Ari butted in, "We're all playing the fool, Uncle, don't get serious. I asked for rooms, you refused. I have the right to spoil your song, don't I?" She came over to the bed with her arms flapping. "I'm a vulture coming to eat you," she wailed like an eagle, "I'm going to eat you, Uncle. Happy?" And we all started yelping like dogs.

Soon she and I were lying flat on our backs on the bed. Kamru sat with his feet up on his chair. Ari brought her palm over my face and clicked a beat with her fingers, an inch from my nose. She started humming, quite by accident, the very song Mother sang in her bath. Kamru tittered as he would to an obscene joke.

I just watched her, eyes wide, shocked at the coincidence. Thoughts raced through my head: was she in on this with Zila and Kamru, what did she know about the tune, about me. My breath grew deeper; I clenched my fists, wanting to get away. I moved around uncomfortably in my skin. *I just heard the tune in my head and Mother's voice telling me to hang the towel on the door. I ignored it. I was under the bed playing a silly game in my head.*

*"Where are you hiding, you filthy pig," she screamed. She couldn't come out just like that as we always had people loitering in the house. "Get the towel!"* Kamru bent forward and looked closely at

me. Ari was singing Mother's song in a nasal made-up voice meant to be funny.

*I ran out. Had I flung the towel at her she would have still shouted at me. I had figured out by then that once she lost her temper, only thrashing me could douse it. I ran out of the house and bumped into Father, who caught me by the scruff and demanded to know where I was off to in the afternoon. Some workers outside were humming my mother's bath song in a seemingly innocent way, but I had heard them talk dirty about her. Mother was always very nice to the workers. Father, the papa of daily domestic brutalities, shook me by the collar.*

*"What mischief have you been up to now?" he asked good-naturedly. The workers sang Mother's song even louder.* Kamru refilled my cup and placed the empty bottle on the table. He kept staring at me.

*"Ma bathing screaming no clothes," is all I could put together, making my father pull me inside the house by my ears. The workers changed the words of the song and sang louder than was needed. Father made me stand in front of the bathroom door while he screamed back at mother shouting filth at me. He called her a whore who couldn't keep her door shut. She flung open the bathroom half-naked and pounced on me. Father threw a towel at her and blocked her path. She wasn't interested in wiping herself dry anymore. He slapped her across the side of the head. She fell in a heap on the floor. He chucked the towel at her again. She just stared*

*at her bare knees breathing heavily. Father left the room, locking the door behind him. Alone, I watched Mother slowly raise herself from the carpet. There was no use running until the deed was done. I waited in my corner and she walked up to a closet under the stairs. I heard the whine of its hinges.* Kamru's breath was two feet from me. I heard a bottle shatter.

*"I'm sorry, Ma," I called out from my corner.*

*She came out from under the stairs holding a small garden shovel the shape of a tight slap. She became somebody else who just wanted to finish a job, and I knew there was no point begging. I waited, my eyes shut. I felt her moist hand clutch mine. The smell of her jasmine soap engulfed me. She led me blindly through the house and I could sense we were heading to the kitchen. She placed my hand on the kitchen table. I opened my eyes as she raised the shovel and brought it down. I forgot to scream. The metal passed a half-inch into my palm. Mother went and sat down on the towel on the floor. I kept standing like that till things got dark and someone shrieked.*

"What do you think you were doing?" I heard Ari's exasperated cry and smelt a cocktail of her sweat and liquor-breath. In a blur, I saw Kamru holding his hand to the light as she wrapped a cloth around it. "Have you gone insane, you drunken bastard, you almost killed him. Look at that hand!" I had smashed the bottle on his hand that glistened red with blood and shards.

The funny thing was that Ari was doing all the screaming, while Kamru and I simply observed her. The broken bottle lay among the broken glass of the tabletop. I rubbed my eyes.

That Kamru had six fractures and fourteen stitches on the hand was not as bad as the news Ari carried out with her: Uncle had lost his head too.

I was deeply bothered by what I did to Kamru's hand. It hurt me so much I slipped into complete vacuum for more days than I can remember. The devotees were told I had taken a vow of silence for reasons best known to the goddess and me. I thought a lot about Nina and when Zila breezed past carrying her flavour, I forgave her for being a nuisance.

My faithful dog's patience perturbed me. Through his drunkenness, he had looked at me with great interest even as his hand was being mummified in shredded bed sheets. He never mentioned the incident again, just hid it in the folds of his brain. He knew he had seen something he should not have and I could not. Silence in return for violence bothers me no end, but I decided I would deal with him another time. I did have a hunch I needed to test, so I asked Zila if she would accompany me in the truck to the other end of town, much to her surprise.

"This is such an honour but, Your Majesty, I

must decline." I asked her why she believed she had the right to refuse.

"If you insist," she said, "I will jeopardize my life for a royal whim."

I swallowed my anger so as not to let her sarcasm succeed. "Get your stuff," I spoke through my teeth, "we will be back by noon." For my part I carried a picnic basket and an old music box. Kamru whispered around her giving instructions till she asked him to relax and await her return.

"I'm not a newborn," I heard her say, "nor have I much more left to lose." I made a sudden appearance and told Kamru to join us on this little outing that I had specially planned for my wife.

"You go, Boss, I was just seeing everything was fine. I'm here. Someone must keep an eye on the house, no? You carry on, I'm fine." He slunk away and we took off for a destination I would decide on the way.

"We haven't spoken in a year," I said, "do you realize?"

She said she hadn't noticed.

"I didn't know the real Kutti was mine."

"You didn't know you kind of raped me?" she looked out of the window. I wanted to strangle her right there for some reason embedded in a corner of my head that controlled sudden unclaimed actions, like that woman of so long ago.

"I was a bit rough," I said, hiding my ignorance,

"but no harm intended."

She cackled, "You kill my daughter and still no harm intended. I am laughing because I don't want to cry."

"Aren't you making this difficult?"

"How's it, Uncle," she still called me that, "that you are going deeper? I heard your heart turns snow to ice. When you start talking like a woman, it makes me nervous."

I glanced at her and knew at once why I must kill her. Zila sat in exactly the same way in the same place in the same truck on the same road as the stranger woman I'd throttled so many years ago. I clung tighter to the steering to keep my hands from wandering to her neck.

"Do you have complaints?" I asked looking straight.

"Not really."

"I treat you like a shoe-brush, even then?"

"Shoe-brush!" she started laughing sadly, "A shoe-brush is luckier, Uncle. A shoe-brush has a face."

"You are angry."

"I'm not ungrateful. You took me in when I was hopeless. Yes, you have tortured me in ways only you understand for reasons only God knows. But I am grateful."

"Why do you whistle before you have something to tell me?"

"Whistle?" she cocked her head.

"Yeah, you and that dog."

She made a face full of confusion and I let the question drop. She cast a glance at the backseat and took an apple.

"You've brought music," she observed.

"Some songs from my childhood. I don't think you have an ear for oldies." She snorted into the second bite of her apple.

"Oldies have a thing for me," she said.

I caught her joke a little late and added, "I liked you."

"Forget it, Uncle, you liked my smell. That's it. I've changed my soap. I'm just waiting for you to stop the car in a secluded part and kill me."

I thought for a while, then said, "Who do you think disfigured you?"

"I know."

I turned my head and saw her looking at me. "No you don't," I smiled to myself.

"I saw Kamru pour the acid," she said. I drove on quietly for another hour before she asked me to stop over a small bridge so she could go under to pee. As a practice, she put on her veil and stepped out in the sun. I sat drumming on the wheel.

What a day to open the can, I thought, she really thinks this is the end.

I had slept off in the warmth of the truck. Zila's knocking woke me up. She slid in smelling of crushed lantana.

"You look sweet sleeping like that," she offered me a palmful of berries. I squished them between my lips just to see her squirm. She wiped the dribble off my chin.

"So why did you come running to me after what we did to you?" I was so damn curious.

"Guess."

"Revenge."

"Another guess, Uncle, this is not a movie."

My nerves were beginning to hurt me tolerating this inane talk. "You thought I'd die soon and you'd have the house and the business," I was serious, but she cracked up. I lost my patience.

I called the guy on the bike that wouldn't let me pass, a bastard. He raced ahead, stopped and parked the bike right across the road, blocking the way. I knocked the ride and the rider out of my path completely and didn't see him get up.

Zila spoke only when we had covered an hour's distance. "This is not a movie, Uncle. What for are you so angry?"

I had cooled down by then. "Why did you come back?" I wanted my answer first. She scratched her chin in an attempt to appear sincere.

"Why did you come back?"

"You can't understand," she spoke with great effort, "you left your heart in the snow."

"Don't let me repeat my question," I begged,

"it makes me so mad."

"Can't you get it, Uncle, I came back for love."

"Acid is love?" I sniggered.

"You disfigured me because you wanted me so badly, I thought. I came back to check and you took me in. You married me for me."

"Really?"

"I said I thought so."

"But you were wrong."

"I guess," she looked directly at me.

"Keep guessing," I said and stopped the truck. We were at the lake I vaguely remembered from my father's stories. It was much smaller though, and drier. I told Zila to spread the food as I walked off looking for a big enough bush to empty out my truth, my bladder.

"I wanted to ask you," I heard her call out, "is this why we are here? To have food by the lake? We could have gone up to the terrace and invited Kamru over to our picnic. Why come all the way?"

I was answering another call and kept her on hold. She went on blabbering till I flopped down on the straw mat somewhere between her and the music box. I put a finger on my lips telling her to shut up. She busied herself in doling out yellow-orange stuff on to the mountains of rice she had served. I turned on the melancholic songs my father made me listen to when I was barely ten. They burned me from the inside. We ate quietly.

Slowly my eyes closed as I drifted off through the pains contained in every heartbeat of the tunes that ran one after the other. I heard Zila say, "Why aren't you eating?"

"I'm waiting for someone," I said.

"Who?"

"A song," I said.

"Let it come when it will."

"I know," I said.

"Some special song?"

"My mother loved it," I said.

"I want to hear that too."

"Of course, you will," I said. And the song mother sang in the bath started playing. I watched Zila as a fear gripped my gut. I tried to soothe my nerves by throwing a glass of water on my head. My hands began to shake. I pulled myself away from the words. My right hand clasped the knife peeping out of the basket. I saw Zila glaring at me and then at the knife. I held her right hand in my left and placed it flat on the straw mat. Zila screamed as I lifted the knife and brought it down on her open palm. She shrieked her guts out. I lurched blindly to the lake and threw myself into it. The cold water woke me up at once. My hunch was right, I stared.

Mother's song made me crush Kamru's hand with a bottle, and Mother's song made me stab Zila's hand. Memory was a bitch, I told myself, and it hounded me like a dog. It made me react in the present to what happened in the past. It wanted me to strangle Zila; it made me knife her. Did they know this before I did? Did they whistle it because they knew? I felt molested.

In the car, on the way back, I told Zila to stop whimpering. Her crude bandages dripped blood on her lap.

"You brought me all the way for this?" she wailed.

"If acid was love, as you said, then this is something far deeper," I told her calmly and drove on.

# *Chapter 29*

On the leeward side of mine, devotees thronged. The house slept little and that too only in the early hours of a new day when the Goddess wore a veil to rest. We had six hours from midnight to eat, sleep, bathe and defecate. Sometimes, Kamru and I wedged in a couple of bottles of liquor. The rest of the business was handled in a collaborative model unique to us - Daya emerged the thinker and decision-maker for the existing channels managed by Bidiya, Chanana and her. She did make an attempt to create franchisees in smaller cities, but the lack of hands-on control burnt her claws. Secretly, everyone was happy at her newly gained humility. I was still the driver of new ideas and rarely ventured into the past, but for monthly collections.

All in all, I had got myself trapped in the respect thing once again and quite often felt outraged by the so-called aura surrounding me. Emarti continued to slyly smile from the necks of thousands of women, some of whom claimed to have seen her apparition. This was a brand new development.

But I now had a problem.

I was erratic with an elephantine 'e'. I was irritated one moment and ecstatic the next. Having Kamru or Zila around calmed me; otherwise the things I said and did could raise an eyebrow sky-high, had I not carried a yellow halo closer to my hair. I, somehow had a feeling this was connected to Mother's bath-song in a convoluted explanation. One night, things got out of hand, quite literally.

I had begun inviting more devotees into the Vulture Room bathroom for a simple reason: to finish more at a time. Four worshippers sat naked across the carpet. I asked them to light the four candles in the corner and they got up one by one and sat down cross-legged again. They were all overweight in varying degrees of lard pouring out of their jowls, arms, barrels and thighs. Their entire life lay before me in the folds of their oversaturated skins, which I had learnt to read. I glanced at their upturned faces waiting for the moment of light. One of them wore a birthmark in the shape of a small country just below the left nipple and it filled me with the warmth of familiarity.

"How can SHE help you," I said, "when you want to follow every word I say?" This honesty always makes the devotee squirm with pleasure, so I continued in the same vein, "Don't listen to me."

The four women stared blankly at me hopeful for more. The mark below the nipple was close in character to Nina's. I closed my eyes blocking out my desperation, but I could hear the sound of morning food travelling down behind the breast of the woman with the birth-stain. I smelled their sweaty scents rise up and conjure images of the nipple. I shut my ears with my hands and put two cotton buds up my nostrils. I remained in that posture until I heard loud whispers grow out of the darkness of the room. I reached out - *I felt two soft breasts filling my palms and the taste of Nina's tongue on mine.*

*"Nina," I cried, "where did you go? I have been bathing alone for so long. Hold me tighter and run your hands through my hair. I like that you know, Nina. Oh, Nina!" I felt fingers tug at my hair and nails dig deeper into my arms and back. I lay down on my back and groaned.*

"He's enjoying it, the swine," I heard a hoarse whisper, "kick him there - that'll teach him!" A chilling pain went right up my spine, killing me. I opened my eyes to four hungry angry faces bearing down on me. The woman with Nina's nipples stood few steps behind. I deduced, not at once, that I was in an awkward situation I had to get out of before news ran out unclothed.

"SHE came upon me," I chanted, "and SHE's hungry. You chased HER away." The four chastened down dramatically, and I told them to go back home and repent for they did not deserve any of this. They settled down at my feet holding back their tears but not their fears, which shone in their eyes. I turned to the one with Nina's birthmark.

"And you," I boomed, "were the chosen one. And you chose to doubt. Put on your pretentious clothes and be on your way. There is no room for the doubtful amongst the faithful. As for the others, you can either follow her at your will or follow HER against your common cow sense," I wasn't too sure what I was expounding, but the effect was quite satisfactory.

The outcast lay amply scratched and prostrate before me while the others begged forgiveness on her behalf. I took my precious time to relent after having thrown a cloth upon her modesty for fear of further urges. My body was listening to my head less frequently, I feared.

"There are only two ways to believe in this real world," I thought up this one just then, "blindly or deafly. But HER way is neither. Her way is through the unreal world where the sorrows of the flesh do not live. There are no judges, for there is no right or wrong. The one thing that exists in HER world is freedom," I looked at the faces that kicked me in the groin, salivating for more, "freedom from one's self."

I caught the still prostrate devotee by the hair.

Her tear-stained cheeks reflected the candlelight. "Do you believe or deceive yourself?" I growled. She cried her intestines out. I ordered her to let her hair lose.

"I'm a sinner," she wept.

"Get down on all fours."

She did.

"Now sweep the floor with your hair." She did so without a moment's hesitation.

She looked ridiculous going around swinging her head like a mastodon. The map of a little country swung with her left breast. At last, I told her to sit down facing me. She obeyed.

"Do you want to experience HER presence?" I asked the group. "Again?"

"Yes," said they in one voice.

I told the three deposits of fat to hold the sinner's arms and chant anything they considered profane. They hesitated. "Free your tongue, free yourself from yourself," I shouted. They started talking filthy the way everyone did in front of the bathroom mirror. Their staccato obscenities became more fluent and fluid. The bodies relaxed from deep within and the breathing became long wistful sighs.

I grabbed the offending nipple and closed my eyes. *Nina came over my shoulder and whispered, "Shall we lie down?"*

I don't remember what happened after, except that I became HER when I wished.

I had created god, or rather, a brand new Goddess. One worshipped only by women. SHE was a doggess as far as I was concerned, but it was for the people she needed a name.

Kamru, Zila and I closed the door behind the last follower on a balmy night and collapsed on the floor. We had not taken a day off since forever, nor could we afford to. Women travelled in groups from places I did not know existed, in the belief that this was where they would find true freedom each one of them had left behind in the first ten years of breast-less abandon. We could not turn them away, no way. The honest truth really was that this sense of godliness was worse than any liquor Kamru could distil on the rooftop. It was more pleasurable than any sacrifice Chanana could invent. If there was a power greater than power itself, this was it. Now SHE needed a name.

Lying flat on the cold floor, Zila and I scratched our heads, Kamru his upper thighs. His fingers were badly repaired and Zila's hand matched his. I had already rejected their branding suggestions meant to please or displease me. I shattered a chair when Zila said the answer to complex stuff was always so simple and if the face of the Goddess was Emarti then the name must surely be Emarti too. It couldn't be Nina either, I warned.

"Then, Boss," Kamru sulked on Zila's behalf, "you created her, you find the name."

"I already have," I exclaimed. I had also discovered in these days the wealth in spontaneity.

"You made us waste our time for nothing, Boss. You always have it your way."

I cared a broad buttock for sentiments and merely laughed at Kamru behaving like a woman of lapsed periods. Zila crawled across the marble till she had her head on my knee. She even barked twice.

"I like to hear your ideas," she murmured, making me suspicious and angry for not being able to tell her fawning from sarcasm. When she licked the air with her tongue, I knew she was merely playing the joker, so I kicked her nuisance a couple of feet away. Kamru grinned at my public display of affection.

"Well...what is it?" he asked.

I let the breathing hold still and said, "Ooee."

"Are you hurt, Boss?"

"That's the name, you mangy dog."

"Ooee?" He said it as if he was making fun of the Goddess and I struck him on the offending lips. Zila stood up defiant.

"That's no name," she protested, "that means nothing. What does it mean?"

"Nothing," I grinned at their ignorance. "It's just a word I invented. Our Goddess is different, so must her name be. What did you just experience when I kicked you?" I asked Zila.

"Pain and anger."

"What have I given you all these years?"

"Pain."

"Why do these women come here and not go to their own?"

"Pain," Kamru joined in getting the drift.

"Ooee comes out of the gut. It is a feeling; it's a cry. And what do we do to this cry of pain? We transform it into the cry of pleasure. And what is this cry of pleasure?"

They chose to watch me ejaculate like an ugly pair of testicles.

"The cry of pleasure is 'Ooee' too," I exclaimed. "We merely change the tune to a freer one. Get it?"

They were nodding their skulls full of null.

"The Goddess shall be called Ooee," I proclaimed.

Ooee had become too big for HER picture frame. A middle-aged divorcee created a life-like bronze of the deity wearing pants and pencil-heels and since we didn't object, she hung a large handbag on HER arm and stuck a pair of sunglasses on HER head. It was only when she was about to place a coiled whip in HER fist that we had her arrested for desecration.

It was, I must admit, Zila's idea to build a temple around the statue and a large compound around that temple. A devotee claiming to be an architect, offered to design, direct and dedicate two years of her life to the work. I had much earlier sent out teams to collect money for buying a hundred acres of disputed land in the heart of the city, upon which the temple was constructed. As a gesture of extreme charity, two quarrelsome brothers gave up their shares in exchange for daily blessings and the special status of being the only men in the congregation. I was so impressed by their generosity that I let them roll around the temple complex in their underwear for free, to gain the Goddess's favour.

By the grace of Ooee and a spot of luck, we had our first white-skinned pilgrim in December that year. She said she was graduating from trekking in the wild to adventure spirituality. "Nice skin," Zila murmured ruefully. I sensed the heat of her hopelessness ten feet away and started watching my back, expecting a jealousy-fuelled attack of some kind.

A rumour sprang up around that time of how Zila was a whore until she met me and to purge her of her past, Ooee had entered my body and burnt her face to render her useless to that profession. This made her feel better and more dignified amongst the community, being the one person so blessed. On being told the story, the white-skinned girl grabbed Zila's breast, as our sign of respect, and Zila came away feeling pleased.

"Nice girl," I heard her say aloud for my sake.

I thought she had settled down within her storm, but I was mistaken. I forgot that people don't so easily forget their slightest instances of having been slighted, and Zila was no stranger to my stern methods of control.

We visited the temple every evening past the daily session at the house. Nothing profound really happened there the entire morning till late afternoon, and we allowed a handful of over-eager volunteers to manage the flow of tourists, tripping over each other for a glimpse of the mute sculpture gazing afar. One day, as we gathered our essentials for the silent evening sit-in, Zila stood over my head. She held my razor in her damaged hand on purpose.

"You don't carry this anymore," she said. "I feel you must today. We have some old friends turning up." Her slit of a mouth curled up to say she was serious and then flattened out to tell me I was free to do as I pleased. Zila had Kamru and Kamru had a nose for news. I took the razor.

"I don't like to be told," I told her flatly, "in return, let me give you some advice. Don't come for the meditation tonight."

She squinted her pigeon eyes, "Why?"

"Did I ask you who was coming?"

"Kamru is right," she was disdainful.

"About what?" I asked so she could get back at me.

"Did you tell me why?" she retorted.

I laughed aloud for her sake. Sometimes, I do these things bordering on kindness not for my soul, but for distraction - Zila did not see me slip the blade into my socks.

"You will not come with us tonight," I ordered her in my voice of finality, choosing not to acknowledge her concern for my safety.

When Daya, Bidiya and Chanana came up to me at the temple steps, I saw ambition swimming in the whites of their wide eyes. They wanted to be where adulation was. I took the razor out and asked them to take it back with them.

"We were here for a more serious purpose," Daya spoke with authority. She had conveniently forgotten the authority the razor wielded in her face at the restaurant. "What can be more serious than my reply," I nodded towards my gift. "It had to go to one of you." Bidiya looked at Chanana for a tenth of a second. Having taught women to free themselves from themselves, I had learnt quite a few things myself and the most sustainable truth was that a woman is a woman's biggest enemy no matter how great friends they are.

"I want you to rotate the razor between you week after week until I stop playing the music. Whoever has it then has it for good," I winked.

Daya opened her mouth again, so I whispered, "The answer is no. Now go." Some answers don't need questions. Any smelly fart could tell they were sick of their bloody businesses and wanted to be a cog in my respect factory.

I prepared myself for a groin-attack that would happen later…just as Zila had predicted.

Apart from overseeing two thousand devotees mill around the statue, the evening was quite uneventful. When it was time to go back to the house, Kamru was nowhere to be spotted. He had taken up the task of driving me to-and-fro as my secretary and soldier. I searched the premises on my own, carrying a small doubt in my gut to keep it from spilling out. I thought I heard the dry cry of a slit throat and rushed to the far end of the property surrounded by wild mulberry trees. Kamru's shirt hung as a white flag from a branch and on it the patches of red screamed loud and clear. I picked up pace.

"Good you came, Boss," I heard Kamru's voice, "I didn't know what to do with this one." He sat in the shade, scratching his bare back. I went over to the spot he gestured with his crooked thumb.

"Help me," I heard a half-scream and looked at one of the charitable brothers trying to keep his head erect as blood soaked him. Beside him waited a freshly dug pit. Kamru kept chasing the itch on his sweaty shoulder blade.

"His brother is inside, Boss, but this one is taking too long. What to do?"

"Did you ask me before doing the other?" I

peeped into the hole and saw him facedown with a flattened skull, probably the work of the broadside of a spade used skilfully.

"They were angry about something."

"Yeah?"

"First they lured them here and then got them."

"They?"

"The girls, Boss."

I smiled a smile of deep worry.

"Bidiya said you left her with a body once, now she's leaving you with two. They had your razor." I could see Kamru slyly gauge my reaction, which I betrayed not. The girls had merely got carried away in their bravado and didn't mean to insult me. I examined the situation.

The bleeding brother started wheezing again. I told Kamru to end his suffering and bury the two fast as we had promised to be home for supper. My brain frowned a couple of creases more, though I was glad I was rid of the two parasites. Obviously, Ooee watched over me.

Come to think of it, by giving me the razor in the morning, Zila had unwittingly killed the brothers, the only male members in the congregation.

Seldom, when I'm by myself, I indulge in a spot of thinking. More than often it culminates in questions being answered by more questions. However, these spasms of thought wander, much against my nature, beneath the surface and far into the depths of things that continue to amaze me: Like why must two lumps of flesh called breasts arouse a man so? Perhaps they remind him of his very first physical pleasure: milk. How is it that every woman then is not aroused by other women's breasts and nakedness as well? Is it because they have seen enough of them - a seller of sweets rarely fantasizes about his own sweets dripping with syrup?

I find it most amusing that most organs of pleasure are also organs of bodily discharge: milk, piss, spit and crap. And interestingly, the act of sex so resembles an act of violence - repeated stabbing, biting, wrestling and at times even drawing blood. Why must a couple indulge in gymnastics to procreate? Does the pleasure born from physical pain free our bodies, our minds? *Were you right, Nina?* Is pleasure, in fact, controlled by the mind? What pleasure is there then, in blood, in pain, in sacrifice and in death? What pleasure is there in killing? It is a hunger; it is a need? Is it why I killed Mother - this need? Is this why anyone kills anyone? *What was your need, Nina. What was your hunger?*

I don't want to go too deep. It makes me mad. The world outside - shallower and holier - was better than the one in my head.

# *Chapter 30*

Good was going great. I got invited to far flung towns to take possession of disputed properties or those of disrepute. The process was simple. I carried my circus to the acres under question and pitched my tent. In a matter of days I had a rough temple to Ooee coming out of the ground, and fresh devotees kept dropping like rain. My jute bag dress had caught the fancy of the youth and girls as young as irresponsibility flocked to be freed. I left a clutch of managers to lead the silent sit-ins every day, when I finally left town. No words were uttered in the temple compound unless they were mine. After the incident with the two brothers, men never entered the hallowed grounds.

I controlled the better half of the world, went the belief.

I was spreading like a yawn, said a local tabloid god.

Kamru was known to have special powers, only in my shadow.

Reports of Ooee sightings sprang out of the blue.

I went into manufacturing extreme satisfaction. My factory was a series of hand-pumps aligned north to south, churning out brackish water claiming to have healing potential. We also set up a bottling plant manned by seventy-four widows and sunk forty new wells in order to catch up on demand. The instructions on the packaging told the customers to boil the contents after adding rice and sugar in exact quantities for a pudding that could free the tongue and all that followed. A few faithful who complained of digestive cramps were told it was their latent energy wanting to break free. 'Faitheal Milk', as the turbid water was called, became big enough for researchers to study its alleged miraculous results.

"I know what this is," bragged one goateed dairy scientist. "It is bad quality water fit for mangroves," and then added with an innocent chuckle, "or womangroves."

"All medicine are poison," I preached to the throngs. A loud cheer rose and fell, with thousands of breasts asking for more. "But even excessive freedom is a killer, as are lipstick and perfume and beauty, if not stopped at the edge of the precipice. You have to stop - even freedom must stop - and you know only when you know." I had discovered the power of spontaneous vomit on a blank canvas. Coming from me, it became art. My utterances could sell anything to anyone because faith had been installed in a huge market of humanity. Meanwhile, the aforementioned scientist collapsed by a coincidence at a conference and my godly status was doubly reinstated.

One day, a man in a very long car came calling. I met him at the gate. Flashbulbs went off like fireworks. Every channel of news carried the picture of the man in jute with his arm around the shoulders of the man in a silk suit. My humility brought tears to the cheeks of civilization.

"You bastard," the man spoke as a ventriloquist would to his puppet, "I'm buying your water even when I know the real scum you are." He waited for a reaction and when I smiled unperturbed, he went on, "My lawyer will settle the deal." He spoke as though the deal was his to settle. I almost snorted, amused.

I took his smug hand in mine and patted it lovingly, "Should I tell these hungry dogs what you just burped? Who do you think they will believe? You came to meet me, not the other way around." I knew what he was trying to do: hook his train on to my bandwagon of devotees. I was nearly impressed by his gall, his shameless approach to business. "Should I tell them you came to donate twenty percent of all you have? Should I say you came to repent for something you did in the early days of your steel contracts and not give away the details? I'll keep the secret in a locker for a later date, okay?" Chess, they say in learned circles, is a very serious game. I feel it is no different from my own verbal ping-pong. The man grinned, "I could have you killed."

"I could kill you myself," I smiled back. The cameras were going delirious at the picture of amity we generated. He laughed good-naturedly.

"I could put a picture of you on every pack," he was a businessman once again, "with a little write-up on your saintly powers."

"Why must you stoop so?" I asked really intrigued. "How can a bottle of dirty water help a man who has everything? What is your greed?"

"Breasts," he said rather seriously.

"I don't have them either, you know," I played along, fully aware of what he was saying. He wanted my women followers to become the followers of his shampoos and other shams. I don't mind brother entrepreneurs - for they are brave men – just as long as their greatness is not at my expense. Their smugness tortures me.

"I could double the offer that man over there has in his pocket." He pointed a thumb at a lawyer-type creature in a black coat waiting for a signal to tapdance hither and get signatures.

"What I don't understand is why you must come all the way in spite of your stature. You could have sent the man with the papers and I would have told him to get lost."

"I'm a great fanatic of yours," he joked, folding

his hands, making the lenses go longer and crazier. I had seen crowds before, but this was a tidal wave. I was being hijacked, I realized, by a snake who had as much interest in milky water than I in Emarti's resurrection. He was already getting the breasts he wanted. His cunning gored me. I felt like hurting his self-confidence, even if it meant slitting my own neck. So absolute was my intolerance of his amiable smile. No one took me for a ride without my consent.

"When they see our picture in the papers," he was saying, "you would have grown beyond your means. Aren't you glad?"

"Let me show you a miracle," I took him by the hand and led him to the sea of paid journalists. He tried pulling out of my grasp, but I put all my energy in gently dragging him along while a slight smile played on my lips. We stood side by side facing the tumbling waves.

"This man you see beside me is a great man." I felt the tug on my arm slacken and I continued, "Not because he has learnt to make money his slave, but for seeking true freedom for the soul in this lifetime. I bow before his goodness."

Next, I asked an important-looking woman in a business suit directly, "Have you the guts to confess your darkest secret?" and not waiting for an answer, I continued, "I don't. But this man in a silk jacket, and a long car I can never afford, has whispered in my ear something he believes is true.

Do you wish to know what he said?"

The multitudes nodded and I let my silence do the talking for a while before I opened my mouth again, "He believes I killed my wife."

A murmur of uncertainty rose in the gathering. They were asking each other if what they heard was what they heard. The man looked at me in utter blankness. His fair skin had turned white. I cleared the air by repeating myself, "This respectable gentleman just asked me if I killed my wife. What do you think my answer was?"

There was a stampede of mikes and a clamour of questions. The lady in the suit got pushed to the ground, her glasses got knocked off and, before anyone could help her up, she was relegated to the dusty fourth row of news-soldiers.

When the noise died down, I turned to he who wanted breasts, "The answer to your question, Sir, is that I did indeed kill my wife."

The dusty woman had rushed to the front. She shouted above the din, "Did you say you killed your wife?"

"Are you stupid or deaf?" I smiled at her as if I would reprimand a child.

"Both," she screamed louder. I liked her.

"Yes, I killed my wife."

I looked to my right and wasn't surprised to see my potential collaborator disappear amongst a huddle of boardroom cowards. I was also, strangely, relieved. It wasn't just the joy of not being manipulated by a smartass, but something much bigger. A huge rock had lifted off my neck. This act of self-immolation was beast of a pleasure.

I was happy I had lost my respect again, however temporarily.

I was sleeping well. A bunch of lawyers was trying to prove me wrong at Zila's insistence. Kamru locked me up in the house. Bidiya, Daya and Chanana stayed away. I asked Kamru to call them for a meeting as I wished to take up the old responsibilities once again only to be told they had taken off for a fortnight. A great many silences greeted me. People were afraid I would blurt out associations of the past, for a man who could give up everything he had ever gathered in a moment was likely to talk. I don't know why no one came enquiring at the house; I expected to be taken away, yet nothing happened.

"Why is everything so okay?" I asked Kamru.

"They don't believe you, Boss."

"Truth is a great liar."

He refused to say anything and sat down on the floor. He saw the expression in my eyes and clarified, "I like the cold marble, Boss. I even sleep on the floor at times without a sheet." I watched him run his finger behind a scurrying large ant and waited for the burst. Eventually, Kamru looked up, pregnant with distress.

"You know what, Boss," he stuttered.

"No."

"I liked the earlier days."

I remained silently watching. He got up and went out and came back again. He held my razor as a dog would a rubber ball. Kamru wrapped the razor in my palm.

"Cut my other ear off, Boss."

"Who gave you that?"

"Found it on the brothers."

A vague thought attacked my gut. The return of the razor was smeared in a disconcerting way. As became my custom, I quickly figured out what I needed to do.

"Cut of my ear, Boss," the dog insisted.

"I haven't lost my touch, Bastard, save your ear for another day. I am not here to please you."

"Tell me to do something real, Boss. Send me to Didoli for a while. Let me clean up my blood. All this chanting and silence has wasted me."

"Get me a finger," I said.

Kamru sat up, "Whose finger, Boss?"

"I don't know. You find out." The dog wanted to play, so I had to throw the ball. No matter what went on in his head all the time, I was still responsible for him.

"I'll be off then," he grinned. I hadn't seen him so happy in a long time. I too, felt a sense of relief.

Zila entered the room only after I had made a

couple of calls to the law. Her face carried a smelly expression.

The authorities dug out the brothers' bodies at the temple. Soon after, Kamru was picked up trying to lure a young girl for the finger I had ordered. I saw him in his cell chatting happily with the tin mug.

He looked up and walked up to me normally, "Don't you worry, Boss, I'm your dog."

"I'm sure," said I.

"I did not name names."

"Good dog."

"I told them I only buried the brothers. I only silenced them because they were in pain. They don't believe me."

"Truth is a liar," I repeated.

"Who called the police, Boss?"

"Them women," I lied.

"Not that I'm complaining, I like it here. But what will you do with them, Boss?"

I smiled at the man's innocence, the daughter of his ignorance. The return of the blade spoke volumes. It had been given to Kamru by the three witches, I was sure, with a promise of huge returns when they seized power from me. Being my dog, he should have given it back to me much sooner. It was a symbol of my status and it is symbols that we live and die for. Daya, Chanana and Bidiya had bribed the fool, I guessed.

"What did they say when they gave you the

blade?"

"I told you I found it." I bored into his eyes and saw no flinching there. Kamru looked back at me as a pet and then averted his gaze with a short honest whine of discomfort, hiding nothing. He had indeed found the blade on his own and was not party to any conspiracy.

"You may die in here, do you realize?" I said.

"I love you, Boss."

I had made a mistake. I should not have sacrificed Kamru.

# *Chapter 31*

Newspaper memory, like the print, is a size too small. The bustle created by the recovery of the brothers' bodies and Kamru's quick arrest died like small pox. My public confession on camera went unnoticed for they tried interpreting my words in philosophical depths and Emarti's disappearance was diagnosed as another miracle. I was again leading the blind in the night-time. The only difference was that those blinded by faith seemed to lose the power of all other senses too, including common sense.

Bidiya, Chanana and Daya paid me a visit in the Vulture Room bathroom. There was a devotee who entered with them for a group session. I was surprised to see them feeling shy of their nakedness in front of me, while the stranger dropped her clothes without a whimper. Chanana whispered into the woman's ear and she promptly gathered her clothes and rushed out amidst pleas of being allowed another chance in the coming week.

"I told her her husband just collapsed," Chanana answered before I opened my mouth, "and she's bothered about the next meeting."

"You will have to be more careful around here," I said. "Now come to the orgasm."

"We want you," Daya sounded certain, "and all of this."

"This," Chanana added spreading her arms. They had decided they did not want years of our building the business to go down the storm-drain. Before any outsider staked claim to my affection, the way it happens in professionally-run corporate houses, the old guard wished to be named heirs. My recent irresponsible streak had been managed with some difficulty and a repeat performance, given my sudden mood-swings, could be suicidal. With Kamru imprisoned for the time being, they had completely forgotten Zila.

"You will need us, now that your snake is gone," Daya's voice quivered in anticipation.

"Dog," I corrected her.

"Of course. Now you have three doggesses," Daya laughed, too loud for the character of the room. Her breasts bounced. That man in the silk suit wanted to control these, I smirked.

Chanana leaned forward, "You think this is funny?"

Daya elbowed her to tame the rage she was nursing. There had been a shift in their demeanour since I last handled them. They were easily angered, but they also had figured out how to cage each other's outbursts. I saw before me a lot of danger. Taking out my razor, I placed it between us.

"Here's the test," I said. "You've failed it once."

They looked at each other to avoid glancing at the acquaintance they had shunned not too long ago. I had earlier made exactly the same offer they now begged from me - the razor would have rotated between them till the day I decided who owned it and 'all this'. Bidiya, who had kept quiet all along, broke her fast, "It was a mistake." She even glared at the other two to tell me without words that she had opposed the decision of dropping my blade in the brothers' muddy blood. Kamru's version - I hadn't forgotten - had been quite contrary.

I slapped my thigh in jest, "Mistake, my nipples. It was defiance. You left the two half-dead for me to finish. You wanted me to be the hyena. You forgot your manners."

"We got carried away," Bidiya persisted in her passivity and this made me suspicious. I had forgiven each of them for a major trespass earlier and, in my eyes, you don't repeat a good deed or it becomes a folly.

"What happens to your business if you take over 'all this'?" I asked Chanana directly to catch her in a weak moment when her eyes were aflame. "Will you sacrifice that?" She was not amused.

"You have moved on too," she muttered.

"But I'm not happy. And I'm not you."

Bidiya, to douse the fire and gain my favour, interrupted with her watered down ambition, "I want to marry." The glare in the eyes of the other rebels told me she hadn't shared this with them. They were annoyed this brought the quality of the dialogue way down low. I wasn't happy either because I thought I had the argument under my thumb and then the stupid melodramatic queen goes and changes the subject. But I am not the kind who suffers soft-hearted ideas in a war scenario with a smile.

"Just produce and let Chanana have them. You don't want that? Don't you want kids, Bitch? Why must you marry? Daya here can get you married every day. Won't you like that anymore? You want to move on."

"Cut the crap, Uncle, we are moving in," Daya became herself, much to my relief. "What do you want from us, be clear."

I pushed the razor towards them, "You just said it."

"I did what?"

"You just said it. Cut the crap."

They looked at me and I pointed to the razor I wanted them to have for good. "Cut the crap," I said again. "Take the test."

"What do you want, Uncle?" Bidiya spoke

softly now. It was clear I was not trifling. I was sure that given their current circumstance, they would succumb to any kind of desperate measure to prove their capability.

"Cut off a breast. One of you," I watched their expressions change direction in a split-second. They exchanged looks.

"Okay, Uncle," Daya spoke finally, "give me a month."

"That gives me a month," I said. I had been wary earlier, now I was worried. Kamru was gone and in that instant I felt the loss panting into my left ear. I depended on my spontaneity for placing obstacles to their greed that were probably possible, yet not possibly attainable. I had to keep their hopes alive, yet hold control - there could be only one Uncle and not three haggling aunties. They were traps disguised as frustrated women, but I wasn't born to be sacrificed.

They whispered like schoolgirls. At last Daya picked up the razor, "Tomorrow, then."

"Two more things," I said, shaking inside. "Bidiya marries Kamru."

Bidiya frowned for a second and then nodded slowly. Her wish granted, I liked the little play here. She was Kamru's whore to begin with and was now going to be his wife. The meaning of life explained in minutes.

"And Chanana," my lip quivered.

"Surprise me, Uncle," she seemed unbothered. I watched her fingers, minus the one I had removed, play with the razor. She pressed her right thumb to the centre of her forehead and left a wet red impression telling me how comfortable she was with fresh blood.

I sounded cool when I told her, "You will give birth to someone's child nine months from now." It seemed preposterous, not to mention paradoxical, that the woman who may have given death to thousands was being requested to give birth for a change. Desperate times call for desperate calls and I knew Chanana was thirsty enough to comply. Bidiya hid a smile in her shoulder. Daya let her lower lip drop like a complaint, having been served a stiffer sentence than the other two.

"Yours?" Chanana asked.

"No. And you will sacrifice the child at your temple on its thirtieth day from birth. Does that sound interesting?"

"Yes," said she. Never in my life had a 'yes' made me so damp near the tail.

As I went to leave for the temple, Zila followed me to the truck that had stuck to my image steeped in raggedness more than simplicity. The discomfort of my jute suit reached such itchy proportions that I flung it at the wall of the vehicle each time I shut the door behind me. Only Zila and the dog observed how I suffered.

"They were here," she mentioned as a passing thought. Since Kamru's departure I had been kinder to her and she reciprocated with her intrusions.

"Very much," was all I told her.

"They are rabid bitches."

"Worse," I said to myself and told her the good news. "Bidiya is marrying Kamru."

Her gait wavered. She held the door of the truck and seemed to admire the dust at her feet. I pulled myself into the driver's seat and gave her time to return to herself. She appeared at the window the minute my patience showed signs of waning. Over the years, she had learnt to manage my volatility of varying degrees.

"I'll stay back today," she was barely audible, "my stomach is weak." She thought for a bit and said, "You haven't left anything to chance, have you? Why must you plan it all?"

"Are you unhappy because Bidiya is marrying Kamru or because Kamru is marrying Bidiya?" I played with fire.

"You are playing with acid, Uncle, you are playing with acid. You already know why I'm staying back."

"But he can't listen to you now."

"You get things so wrong at times. I am not rushing to the prison; I am running away from you. I don't want to burn my face again for nothing."

"Hop into the truck," I ordered.

"And get into the muck?" she asked.

The spotted dog I'd seen loitering around came wagging its tail at Zila and proceeded to pee on the front tyre. *The smell of first rain on a dusty plain, but with urine flavour, arose. A bitter juice began rising in my gut and a burnt tobacco smell wafted in through the open glass. I heard singing in the back of the truck with a lot of stomping on the wooden floor.* Zila was staring at me from outside. For the first time, I became acutely aware of my simultaneous realities. I knew this was a dream from the past I could do nothing about except, bear the pain till the mind wore out. It was as though I was watching a vision from the past seep deeper into the present until it engulfed it, and me, whole.

"Are you coming in or not?" I growled, clutching the lard around my belly. *The drunkards in the back were making a ruckus that drilled my brain and drummed my ears. I felt a whack at the space below my head and the cabin whirled around crazy. I wanted to puke the bitterness out.*

"I wish you suffer," I heard Zila cry somewhere in the dark.

*A hand pulled me out by the hair. I was thrown to the dust and the stomping went on all over me. I felt boots crush my ribs and heel my guts. A warm smelly tap opened on my face and when it stopped two more streams of urine bathed my eyes and nose and ears. I heard laughter dancing all around me. The kicks started.* Remnants of a long-forgotten truck ride rocked my mind.

*"Take his clothes off," a loony voice screamed.*

*They grabbed my hair again and ripped open my shirt. Hands struggled with the pants and began beating me, tearing me to shreds. A man said 'owwwaaaah' and showered me with vomit. My insides were churning up. He said 'awaaaah' this time and filled my hair with undigested liquor and morsels of meat.* Panicked, I threw up all over me too.

A whistling opened my eyes to Zila leaning in my face. I was lying flat inside the truck and she bent over me, whistling a tune of the hills. The tune reminded me only of Nina; it froze her in time, it was the tune I sometimes whistled when I thought of her - the tune of a faraway flute. *I could smell my vomit but also smelled the fragrance of freshly cut grass.* I was torn between what was real and what seemed real - the visions were multiplying around me. *I expected a cow to graze my shoulder with her jaw and nuzzle my neck. I chuckled, "Stop it, you." It licked my ear wet, making me push it away. I was laughing as the sun bore down gently on my tousled hair. A faraway flute played the same old song and then suddenly stopped. I panted.*

"Better, you piece of filth?" Zila was saying.

I sat up. My jute suit and the truck seat were a mess.

"Go back in and change," Zila snapped, "I'll

get this graveyard cleaned."

"Keep whistling," I told her, "I feel good."

"I know," she said under her breath.

"Then keep whistling," I caught her arm. She pushed me away. I watched her wipe the seat with my costume. She began humming Mother's bath song instead, just to spite me. I gritted my teeth. She stopped abruptly and smiled like she controlled my breath. The faraway flute from a little expedition I took with Nina in the hills made me happy and calm, whereas Mother's song or any song Mother loved just made me mad - Zila knew this full well. The other three had no clue what powers she alone possessed. She whistled and I wagged my tail, she changed the tune and I howled in agony.

"Disturbing?" she patted my head in the manner of an unsmiling schoolmaster as she jumped off the pukeworthy truck. She was obviously aware of the effect she had on me. I let my right hand hold my left and hit it against the dashboard twenty times. How hard Zila's brain struck the insides of her skull on hearing the news of Kamru's impending wedding, I had no desire to dwell upon just then.

Having had enough of the four women for the day, I skipped the temple in the afternoon. Instead, my legs took a short walk and left me staring in front of an iron gate, the only weak spot within a very tall wall, garnished with embedded glass and barbed wire. I had never returned to my blind school in almost ten years. The watchman of blind men and boys greeted me and let me in without a word. I liked that.

It was lunchtime, and the ground and the crumbling classrooms were deserted. I could hear the clamour of pots and plates jostling with the noise of sightless voices. The stench of rice and sour curd was still revolting. I never had the stomach for blind food and always went home for lunch, first to Nina's equally bad cooking for twenty years and then to a dour Emarti for the rest of her mortal life. I had no desire to talk to the masters or anyone else, and took myself up the brick steps to the roof. I saw a boy of fourteen sitting near the edge, smoking. He seemed to be looking into the distance. I leaned against a half-drum half-filled with white lime meant for the walls and forgotten.

"What do you see?" I asked after a while.

"Everything."

"But you can't."

He blew smoke like a grown-up, "I can hear, smell and feel the past."

I descended the stairs and left the compound. There was not much difference between the blind boy and me. I closed my eyes and walked back home feeling the air with my tongue.

"Such a snake," Zila hissed close to my ear, reminding me of what she thought of me after the events of the day.

# *Chapter 32*

Betraying no sadness by virtue of her flat face, Zila unlocked the rooms at the house. She turned Kamru's room and the two on either side of it into a comfort zone. I was astonished nothing emerged from under the beds when she bent down and reached out with her broom. The housekeeping people had long abandoned us and it was Zila who orchestrated the innards.

I had made it clear that their moving into the house would need all three to keep their word absolutely. A month passed. Kamru was to marry Bidiya on a Wednesday night – we had also decided to keep the temple closed that day. Daya's breast would have healed from the surgery she had decided upon instead of a quick swipe of my blade. Chanana could still not find anyone to consummate the remaining promise. I failed to understand why she was so particular about quality since the outcome was to eventually be sacrificed. Every man in a radius of ten miles was at risk. Her eyes checked each product on two legs as a bored wife would the items in father's grocery store.

"Found the sacrificial wolf or what?" I caught her off-guard one morning. She had been pacing up and down the steps leading to the central hall at the temple.

"You know a lot," she said out of breath.

"These people," I waved a hand at the women swaying silently to the tunes in their heads, "believe I have certain powers. What takes you so long?"

She curled up a lip.

"Ready by Wednesday?"

"Four days should be fine" Her voice was uncertain.

"What took you so long?"

"You've become a woman, Uncle. Just look at yourself. You want to get into details, the gossip. I bet you have an udder under the sack. Whose idea?"

"My robe?"

"Your shroud," she laughed. I had to shut her up just as a clutch of devotees from some obscure village fell at my feet. I held each one of them, looked them in the eye and sent them off to meditate in the hall. The clutching of breasts was a more personal blessing and it happened only in the bathroom at the house or in the shadow of Ooee's statue. An architect, who was actually a politician with a sculptor father, had taken over the responsibility of multiplying the statues across the city. He seemed committed as a great many devotees meant good commerce.

"Who is the choice?" I asked Chanana.

"I wish it was you," she replied with a devious chuckle emphasizing my age and, therefore, my agility in bed. Given her predisposition, she could insist on making babies on a stone slab, which would definitely not suit me. I believe even the act of sacrifice was almost orgasmic for her because it entailed a spurting of bodily juices. I considered her comment.

"You want to shed my blood," I nodded sportingly at her attempt at humour at my expense. She took a step back and let it pass. I guess, she realised her own ability to procreate was borderline, and did not want me venturing there. She was neither a beauty nor bad. But at somewhere between sixty and sixty-five, her sinewy trunk and branches held an unquenched desire to flower. At least, so I thought, she was certain of her fecundity.

"Have you ever reproduced?" my own words surprised me. She had been waiting for this.

"Yes," she said simply enough to shock me. "Twice," she added like seasoning.

"What became of them?"

"What became of yours?" I could tell she had been talking to Zila or Kamru on the subject.

"I ate them."

"Her, you mean."

"I don't remember details."

"I have a son," she held on to the pause too long as if she was deliberating the next bit. At last she sighed, "I had two sons. One died in birth. I don't know his father."

"Where's the other?" I asked.

Chanana laughed. The entire property shook. She caught her breath with a hand on her chest and pierced me with a million pins. Her hand trembled, I noticed.

"The other son?" I prompted carefully.

"He's in prison, Uncle." She had a twitch coming up near the left eye. Her voice carried the reverb of a hundred elephants. A darkness descended all around her.

"Do they know?" I asked of the other two witches.

"No," her jaw tightened, "they don't know my son is getting married on Wednesday to one of them."

The steps slipped out gently from under me. Kamru was Chanana's son, it was all so clear. He took me to her and she bit the lump off my neck. By inviting her to the storm-drain to look for babies, he was doing his mother a favour. It was all so clear. If she was his mother and Sattu's whatever, and she bore him at thirteen, she should be way beyond seventy with little chance of giving birth. Chanana could not pass the test no matter what concoction she put in her milk. Their plan would fall because of her failure.

Eggs fell into the tray, still I refused to stray. Chanana had to keep her promise. Wednesday came and went. Kamru married Bidiya in the jail within ten minutes. They shared a quiet cell for a few days because I could make things happen. Daya recovered fast, but Chanana had no hope even two months after.

She had chosen, chased, abducted, loved and almost killed two of the seven men she considered most capable to copulate with and yet, she remained unscored. I would not budge. Someone of Chanana's make has venom coursing through the veins and that she could still beget a child, was my belief. She could sacrifice a newborn and change her fortune.

"You know it's impossible," Daya told me angrily.

"Sacrifice your ambitions then."

"We have done what you wanted. She tried, didn't she?"

Bidiya had become quieter since her wedding, so it was Daya who carried on.

"She will sacrifice ten if you want," she blabbered.

"Not her own. Not her own." I had the upper hand and I held no desire to forego the advantage. Chanana sat in the corner watching me perform.

"A commitment is granite. You know me," I said.

Chanana stirred from her perch. "Let's go back," she said. I laughed inwardly at their helplessness; this was not a game for the weak-hearted.

"How the hell can I get back!" Daya screeched thumping her chest. "Even she can undo her slut-wedding to that thing," she pushed Bidiya away, "but how can I get my breasts back! Can you get your bleeding back?"

I was enjoying this turn of fate. Chanana still looked at me, pleading silently, hoping to touch some hidden wire in my soul. I walked to the door.

"I swear I'll destroy you, Uncle," Daya screamed behind my back. I turned around to hear her out. She cooled down as a bitch dripping with a bucket of water on her head.

"Where's my razor?" I asked quietly. Bidiya went out briefly and came back with it. I gave it to Daya. "Destroy me," I said, as I had on another occasion.

She held it gingerly. I told her to open it. She hadn't heard, it seemed. I did it for her and held it to her cheek. I asked her how she wanted to destroy me. She didn't hear that either. So I ran the blade from her ear to her chin in the shape of a very thin moon spouting red. She didn't bat an eye. I liked that.

"There's a way," I announced, pocketing

the razor. Chanana glanced up. Daya remained motionless.

"Yeah, Uncle?" Bidiya chirped. I was sure I was making the mistake of my life.

"Chanana must sacrifice your baby." I dangled the idea mid-air like bait.

"I am not," Bidiya stammered.

"Kamru told me you are expecting a visitor," I said coldly watching Chanana.

Her expression changed to a moonless night. I could hear people screaming in the tunnels of her mind. Bidiya stared at her hands.

"Great," Daya spoke without a clue of what I was actually suggesting.

"I'll do it," Chanana called from her corner, her grandmotherly emotions overtaken by duty. I got the feeling, from her quick yes, that the revelation about her relation to Kamru was nothing but well-timed and deliberate.

Bidiya thought forever and said nothing, meaning she was trapped.

# *Chapter 33*

I had only one reason to get myself into trouble again: sheer pleasure. The extreme risk embedded in my offer excited me greatly. I had already thought of the next level. I was almost certain of the ultimate pleasure, but it was these in-between steps I found difficult filling with my inventiveness and upgrading of thought. I knew who murders the landlady, it was the rest of the story I had to painstakingly fill. It was a chance remark by Zila I had to thank this time.

She now had a family of five to think of. Not counting Kamru and his unborn child, of course. At her insistence - because she had cleaned the rooms, so it seemed, with her tongue - I had become a bit lenient and allowed the three doggesses into the house even though only two of the promises had been executed. Zila guaranteed me the third would follow the birth of Bidiya's baby. She hadn't foreseen the darkness they were capable of breeding.

"How will you curb their desires," she ventured

one day in the truck. Incidentally, it was in the truck that we had our conversations. Since Kamru's departure, I gave Zila a little more ear and lip.

"Chanana needs blood. Is there a way to keep her happy? I was sitting in the hall with her the other day and she was telling me about this place in the hills. Are you listening?"

I told her I was totally there, just a trifle preoccupied.

"So I was listening to her talk with such relish about the trees and the cliffs and the birds. She had shut her eyes imagining, I believe, a god was making love to her. You there?"

I gave her a cold stare, "Hurry on with it. You aren't anybody yet." I wanted to say 'Nina', but my teeth held my tongue. I had been pondering over not having visions of her as often as I did. Having four women in the house probably pushed her into a corner. The thought made me angry.

"I was sitting listening to her," Zila continued unmindful of my tone, "and her hand started touching me. Her eyes remained closed like she was in a very pleasurable dream. She put her hand on my thighs and began massaging me all over. And she was murmuring to herself."

I became more interested. Nina's memory again moped in a corner. Zila had found a way of gaining my attention, I noticed. But I could not tell what went on behind her acid-face.

"She touched my belly, my breast, my nose, my ear and then when I was beginning to get annoyed, she touched my neck. I felt fear, Uncle. I swear I started sweating. She merely stroked my neck and I was sweating buckets. I just sat quietly while she moaned in some sort of orgasm."

The idea for the next level had already hit me.

Zila said, "Chanana was imagining a sacrifice. She was fiddling with my vein. Her greatest pleasure was cutting my neck. She needs a diversion, Uncle."

I didn't say anything. I needed one too.

Little did I know that I was going to practise a higher plane of pleasure that day itself.

A dark-skinned rough-haired wife of a middle-aged art-collector sat across cross-legged. She had dots of darker skin near her nipples and upper thighs.

"Burns. Cigarette," Chanana whispered over my shoulder. I had asked her to be with me in the sitting as the diversion Zila spoke of, I suppose.

The woman heard her and nodded. She wore a solemn mask though her eyes watered. I told her to light the candle and she got up wearily displaying a hundred more tattoos inscribed by a man close to her. The ones on her buttocks were fresher and redder from the ointment she had anointed herself by looking backwards into a full-length mirror.

I felt Chanana's hand on my shoulder and

shook it off. The woman sat down again.

"What he wants from you," I opened my gob, "is not important. What you want is."

"What do I want?" she asked stupidly.

"Freedom." It's true, I was getting bored of repeating the same old freedom-song. Chanana craned her neck like an artist's over-attentive apprentice. I had the urge to flip open my razor and create a necklace of glistening red beads around it.

"I am free to leave him when I want," the woman argued with her own thoughts gently.

"Are you really? Can you walk out of this room and never go back to him? Do you have the freedom to do that?"

She contemplated for a while longer than I expected. An itch from the jute bag was fingering a spot near my shoulder blade. I tried to reach it, but it was too far out. Chanana's fingernails began scratching it to a degree of pleasure. I thought of Kamru and reminded myself of their shared blood.

"Guess not," the dark woman said finally.

"Why?"

She displayed ignorance.

"Because there is no pleasure in walking out. Not pleasurable enough. What is it you want?"

She was as clueless as any devotee who walks into my presence. The reason they are there is their cluelessness coupled with the willingness to be buffaloes; the bovine eyes begging to be milked.

My father took me to a settlement of nomadic cowherds when I was ten. A youngish woman who smelled of curd took me to her straw hut to show me a newborn calf. I pulled the animal's ear and loved the sound it made, but it was its mother's story that intrigued me for many months thereafter.

The gypsy made me sit in her lap against her bare bosom. Even at that age, there was joy in those nipples touching my ears. Two mounds of flesh could be so pleasurable. And then she told me the story of her buffalo.

It so happened that the animal, which gave milk twice a day, had suddenly turned dry in the evenings. They thought there was a thief and they kept watch for outsiders, but the buffalo gave not a squirt in the evening. The morning buckets ran full.

The community believed there was a thief amongst them, so they kept vigil over the barn. The story repeated itself. A full udder at three was empty at five and not a drop was dropped. The lady I sat upon spent the next day and the next and the next sleeping almost under the udder. It was then she discovered a truth about buffaloes. They believed blindly in what they were made to believe.

When she was watching the four teats, she heard an inaudible rustle in the straw-pile. A snake raised its head oblivious to her presence and touched its lips to the buffalo's muzzle. Then it glided through her mesmerized front hooves and wound itself around the hind legs. My narrator saw the serpent drink milk from one teat at a time till it was bloated, and lay there quietly digesting its kill. The buffalo needed the serpent and the serpent needed the buffalo for some unexplained purpose.

I looked across at the woman contemplating emptily and imagined myself as the serpent. I needed the devotees for my fill of pleasure borne out of their absolute submissiveness as much as they needed their hypnotist.

By the way, Father went to the nomads' huts for the very same reason: pleasure.

"What is it you want from the man who burns your butt with cigarettes?" I asked the woman again.

She only pretended to think.

"I'll tell you what," I pushed her to the brink, her eyes shut and ears peeled. "You want to burn his butt."

She went into one of her silences. Normally, I finish cases very fast and four at a time, but this was a new experiment in euphoria, so I waited.

"Yeah," she sighed. As if every bone in her body relaxed, she breathed in long bursts from her open mouth. She had had egg and pickled pork in the morning.

"You want to tie him up on a slab of ice and hot-brand him."

"Yes."

"You want to take a knife and carve pictures of hell on his arms and chest."

"Yes."

"You want to cut off his ears, chop off his nose, lop off his thing and string them around your neck."

"Yes. Yes." She was orgasmic.

"You would love to kill him."

"Yes.", she cried.

"But you can't."

"Yes," she toned down suddenly back to reality after the ejaculation.

"But you want him worse than dead. You are not bothered about your own life, you want freedom. And you'll be free when he suffers. Is that so?"

"Yeah," she wiped the sweat on her forehead.

"But if he suffers, he'll hit back," I was treading carefully now. Chanana's breath was warm on my neck. I was on a merry-go-round, my heart thumping like a circus drum. "What if you disappear?"

"He'll find me," she said, her eyes filled with terror at the prospect of being found hiding in a manhole. I reached out and grabbed a breast violently, she looked into my eyes. I eased my grip and gently stroked her. She moaned like the buffalo.

"He won't find you if you are really free," I talked in the voice of a father. "He won't find you if you are not there."

Her eyes asked 'how?'

"Die," I whispered. Blood had rushed to my head. The very sound of the proposition made my heart race. The prospect of such a vengeful finality shook me. I looked at her, appearing calm. She placed her hands on the floor, supporting herself. The buffalo and the serpent were one. She fell back satiated.

My head was spinning. I heard a voice calling out, "Uncle." Chanana was tapping my shoulder. I raised a hand to tell her to keep her trap tight. The woman stirred. Very slowly she raised herself back to the cross-legged position.

"Sorry," she murmured. I smiled kindly. "How does one die?" she asked innocently.

"Wrist. Cut your wrist," I advised, "it is louder than a gun. Write a letter implicating the bastard. Do it in the bedroom when he is asleep beside you. He won't hear a thing. You won't feel a thing. You will find freedom in your sleep. He can't ever catch you."

"Will he suffer?"

"Many times more than you have," whispered I. Chanana nodded behind me. Her eyes were delirious. There was a delicious odour in the room.

"When is a good day?"

I stared into the candle flame in the corner and said, "Four days from now. Friday night. Enough time to say good-byes. Meditate in silence the whole day and look at each scar on this beautiful body gone ugly."

"How should I cut my wrist?" she was now going into stupid territory, trying my patience. Chanana placed a burning hand on my shoulder. I took my razor out and showed it to the ignorant fool, without a word. She understood perfectly.

Four days later, Chanana brought the news: the woman was found plastered on her bed, in coagulating blood. Chanana placed a quivering hand on my lap. I had an arousal.

# *Chapter 34*

Surprise became me. Sixteen identical suicides in the bedrooms of the city in four months, and no one connected them to my looking pleased with life in general. Zila accosted me in the bath, the only place other than the old truck where she had my antennae.

"Aren't we overdoing it," she kept her voice low.

"We?" One word was sufficient to curb her excrement, so I reckoned. She merely smiled sadly at the obvious nature of my attempt at deflation.

"I thought you were fifty people," she had learnt to be freer in her toxicity in the permanence of Kamru's absence. Her sarcasm had gained higher levels of alkalinity.

"Cut to the song and dance," I spat out.

"Too many cut wrists. Too many convictions."

"The dead deserved to die and their living deserved to suffer."

"You're God, I forgot," she persisted in tackling me.

"I'm not God," I said throwing on my jute bag,

"I created God or rather, a Goddess. What is it you want now?"

"You haven't been too kind to women yourself. What do you say to setting example?"

"Are you entertaining me, Bitch? How would you like to be found clotting in bed? I could make a damn good example," I said, wanting to end her nagging, "What is your problem who dies? Just enjoy the show, okay."

"How about a little restraint? Or we'll have trouble at the doorstep. How about a little control, Uncle? Don't go senile yet."

I grabbed her throat and made myself clear, "Don't get any lofty thoughts. I am not here for your ego-enhancement or your flat-faced sentiments. Give me another chance and I'll fill you with geese feathers of inferior quality. Go."

She took gulps of air and crashed down on the plastic bath-chair I had begun to use in secrecy with the advancement of my years. She gathered herself up and brought her nose in line with my chin. I smelt Nina. I missed her suddenly.

"Let's begin by controlling our anger, Uncle." Zila thrust a wet embroidered cushion she had carried inside in my face. I had told her a story about it in a weak moment, I recalled. *An icy pain went down my vertebrae. I heard Father's voice telling me to 'spit it out'. I felt suffocated by a mustiness of silk.*

*"You want to throw dirty words at your mother,"*

*he yelled, pressing my face down on the couch. "How many you got there in your stinky mouth? Spit it out, spit it out." He had poured cubes of ice down my back and sat on me to cool me down.* Zila flattened me against the wall. I could not move my hands. The smelly cushion suffocated me.

*"Get off me," I cried.*

*"Spit it out first," Father kept repeating, "spit out every dirty word you have on your filthy tongue. You want to get angry? Let me cool you down once and for all." The ice was burning me more than anything else. But Father wouldn't let go of a chance for such physical forms of education.*

*I spat out I don't know what. "I'm sorry," I sobbed, "I won't call her a bleeding bitch again." I know I didn't mean a word.*

*"You just did," father was no fool. He remained on top of me saying, "Spit it out, spit it out." The cushion under my nose smelt of the dog's pee. I passed out.*

I found myself on the bathroom floor in my jute suit, and Zila sat beside me holding my hand. The floor was cold, my back hurt. The cushion sat on the chair, assessing me innocently.

"Feeling better, Uncle?" she asked. I wondered what had just hit me. Zila helped me up. She even started to whistle the faraway flute melody I had liked in the truck. *I expected a cow to lick my ear and it did. I smiled.*

"Let's go to work now," her hand patted mine.

Yes, ravaged was the word. I remembered being absolutely helpless on the floor. Zila had turned me into a lab rat, and carefully noted down all the stimuli I responded to either vigourously or amiably and, under the guise of guiding me, let my emotions rape my body. She took charge of me and repeatedly reminded me to keep my anger caged or I'd die. I wasn't scared or anything, I just had this sense of peace when Zila hung around. Watching her whistle to herself made me feel good about me. Zila replaced Chanana in the bathroom sessions after an incident I don't recall too well.

Bidiya was bloated up and was due anytime. I saw the three and Zila huddled together more often than I recommended. Bidiya remained anxious and Chanana's bravado seemed to dilute. She had lost her craving for the knife, I could see. I expected a delegation to confront me with a message of forgiveness soon. Daya remained somewhat aloof, though she had forgotten her own sacrifice to a great extent. Chanana wanted to continue accompanying me in the hope of coming closer and, therefore, closer to reprieve from executing her promise made nine months ago. But Zila had her own logic - of controlling me - in occupying her place behind me in the Vulture Room bathroom.

Chanana refused. We were at the lunch table, if I'm not misplaced. Chanana and I. Zila called from the kitchen, "I'll be going with Uncle for the sessions now on."

"My foot you will," Chanana replied.

"Let her, Bitch," Daya came out of her room rubbing her hair vigorously. She had contracted lice and the nurses at the hospital cut her hair to an inch off the scalp making her look manlier than she already was. Her demeanour, however, had become more lumpy than consistent.

Chanana glared at her and fiddled with the butter-knife meaningfully. I found the exchange very amusing and continued taking small bites of whatever. Zila placed a bowl of sweetened rice to finish the meal with. She also told Chanana, in as many words, to stay home and sharpen the knives.

"Watch your mirror-face," Chanana fumed. Zila casually began humming something, softly at first. I realized it was Mother's bath-song. *The aroma of the sweetened rice was nice. Someone pinched my ears, I looked up. It was my imagination.* Zila hummed louder.

My throat went dry and my hands shook as I lifted up the jug to refill my glass. "You okay, Uncle?" I heard a voice say. Zila continued whistling. I gulped down water. *An old fear rose inside my ribcage wanting to burst out.* I snatched the butter-knife out of Chanana's hands and threw it across the room. I was fighting off Mother's song. The walls were spinning. I stood up. I felt a pair of hands holding me and Chanana's voice said, "Here,

Uncle, sit down."

I held her hand and thrust my spoon through her palm, cracking a million bones. Daya threw the jug of water over my head on Zila's instructions. Chanana fell to the floor writhing in anger and disbelief. I sat down on the chair bathed in despair.

Zila had proved her point - she could control my emotions as and when she wished. Chanana let Zila accompany me thereafter. I'll make a technical observation here: Zila was my heir by marriage in the whore business, she was a nobody in this spiritual pimping. Her flashes of heat were totally justified because she feared what should have been hers was being carefully hijacked by the three doggesses.

Like I said, Zila's presence comforted me in a Nina sort of way. I even called her Nina on the terrace at the start of a private session for a very important lady with an entourage.

"I imagined her name was something else," the famous singer poked her nose in, unnecessarily.

"You may call me Something Else," Zila laughed behind her veil. From being Nothing when I first met her to becoming Something Else was quite a transformation.

"Well, Something Else," the retarded woman carried on pompously, "why the veil?"

Zila went over to her and kneeled down, "Because I am Something Else behind. Would you care to see my face?"

I barged in, "Let's all go down." I began descending the steps and Daya and Chanana followed me.

"I shall bring the lady," Zila called after us. I was surprised and amused at her overt reverence. That she wanted people to see her ugliness, spelt something I could not place a finger on. I saw my escorts looking at me.

"She's domesticated you, Uncle. You're losing your touch," Chanana cribbed. Daya nodded in a non-committal way. I fingered the razor in my pocket.

A loud cry ripped the air.

"Zila has shown her true face," I commented happily. I was generally happy with her for a deeper reason too: she kept the doggesses on a long leash after her supremacy over Chanana.

No more suicides were reported since Zila took over my temperament. Bidiya's day drew nearer. Chanana's fears were written across her darkness. And Daya basked in the shadow of underlying confusion. They were quite sure of the onset of my dementia, and I let them believe.

I let Kamru know of Chanana's dilemma. He shrugged his shoulder with a normal, "Don't let me see the kid, Boss. The rest is your business. I'm still your dog." Though my dog had hidden a few bones too many behind my behind, I trusted him more than all those lying bitches.

Bidiya was rushed to the doctor fifteen days too early. Kamru was not told. I remembered the day that gave birth to Kutti - how he ran out to get a baby for a baby. Yeah, he was my dog in his kennel now.

Bidiya had requested Zila by her side for the very reason Chanana and Daya obeyed her - Me. I controlled Ooee, and Zila controlled me. The revelation jostled me as I strolled along the corridors of medicine. Zila was the silent serpent and I the ruminating buffalo. Something else struck me that moment: the smell of formaldehyde and toxic memories.

*I had the urge to hide and laugh and hide a laugh. A pair of fingers touched me in the ribs and I turned around bursting at the seams. "Stop it," I told the guy with the buck teeth. He showed me his fingers and tickled my sides. The biology teacher was somewhere in the racks. I muffled my laughter with both my hands. Chari went on prodding me with his fingers. "Get off you bastard," I cried, "they will find out." He went wild. Four more hands tickled me mad. I burst out and they kept on tickling. My stomach was aching, my tears were running, my jaws were locked and I was whooping and crying like a maniac on the floor.* The hospital floor was cold marble. The white lights dazzled me. I saw many faces bearing down on me not daring to touch. The smell of formaldehyde was suspended low in the air. My back hurt. *They didn't leave me. I shouted obscenities at the top of my lungs. They got more violent and I knocked off the brains stored in glass jars. The smell of formaldehyde was all over me, eating me and they didn't leave me. I was burning and snorting and sobbing all at the same time. I peed in my pants and they stopped. They made fun of me. I pulled myself into a corner. They ran away. I fell asleep in my biting skin.* A lot of people were creating a ruckus. Shoes squeaked close to my ear. A patter of high heels went running away. Someone was whistling.

*I opened my eyes to the smell of freshly cut grass. A cow licked my ear. I felt nice. The sound of a flute far away made me float.* I felt a hand on my head.

"Uncle," Zila said, "it's okay. I'm here." I glanced up at her sitting on the floor beside me.

"Give him water," I heard Daya say and looked around. Chanana was also bending over me showing off her wrinkled breasts. Some other creatures too stood away a bit. I asked Zila for more. Only she understood and started whistling the cow-tune, and I drifted off to sleep on the hospital corridor floor. They told me later that I slept for three hours. Bidiya's son and Chanana's grandson was born in the meantime, ready for sacrifice.

Kamru's request being kept, no one visited him for a month. We all packed up and went to Didoli instead. Zila said I had forgotten Nina and

I thanked her for reminding me, but I was certain she had a motive far superior in taking me to her.

Didoli was always a comma in my life. I realised, I hadn't rested in years and the fresh mountain breeze ran its fingers through my hair and beard, like Nina would have, comforting me greatly. I saw Nina in every cornice. It was she who walked with me, talked to me, bathed me and woke me up in the middle of the night to silently sit on the rock by the gate. My eyes rested and my ribs relaxed. I told Zila what an excellent idea this was.

So who did I trust with the running of the temple while we were away? No one but the locks. We shut the doors for two weeks because, as Zila brilliantly suggested, Ooee went off to sleep in those days in the year. The visitors and volunteers were advised rest in imitation of HER. Zila always came up with answers that the others questioned in their own spaces. I let her share Nina's room with me. Chanana stayed with Bidiya and her grandson, and Daya wafted in and out of the living room where her cot occupied a corner near the window. The baby's laughter lived with all of us. I could say we appeared a family come to see the mists rise from our minds.

Zila took great pains with my memories of Nina. She asked me about the things she said, and the habits she had. I felt transported to my days of abandon because Nina was everywhere, and I had nothing on my head. Zila found her stuff all over the house and I told stories of my boy-days to which she listened with a smile, never envying my stepmother, the only woman I ever loved. Would I have forgotten her had the trip not happened? Maybe she had been getting lost all this while in the vagaries of my other memories.

The women cooked and I watched the kid kicking the air. Bidiya came over every now and then to cast a glance and chatter stupidities. The baby stayed in a cradle with wheels that could be pushed around the house except where I sat. I was fine with that. I could not stand the smell of urine-soaked cloth. It made me angry and sad, which was not the idea of coming to Didoli. I smelled a lot of Nina though, and became acutely aware they were all using her soap to make me feel good.

Two weeks flew past. We returned by train without a word. As it descended through the tea gardens, my spirits rose. I saw certain things in greater clarity, back to being myself. For instance, I found Zila sitting too close to me for comfort. I gave up my seat to her and walked over to the next coach. No one knew me there, of course, I wasn't in my jute suit.

"Have I seen you somewhere?" a stylish man smoking at the open door enquired. The wind blew his ashes back on to his grey silk shirt, giving the appearance of dander. I don't like smugness in people who can't carry it off.

"In your mother's petticoat perhaps," I told him only to shake him up for his own good. The razor nestled in my palm making me feel godly after a long break. I don't know if the man was sensible or a coward in his silence. The diesel fumes from the engine replaced the mountain mist in my lungs.

The day of the sacrifice came sooner than I expected. Little had happened in the countdown, but for Zila's perpetual presence. I begrudged her controlling me by some invisible force, yet her whistling or humming or doing things around me made me feel warm. I let me be.

We travelled to the temple of the altar in the truck, all six of us. Zila, the baby and I in the cabin, which meant the three bitches lurched about in the back. Zila made the baby touch my face and made nonsense sounds that irritated me. I smiled at Kamru's son once, but keeping up the farce was not my cup of cheer. We were constantly treated to Bidiya weeping, through the hole in the wall behind us. I wanted the show to get over fast, so we could all go home and have mutton and rice. The night crept around making a black and white movie out of us.

"He doesn't even know," Zila broke the gurgling in the air. I had no clue whom she spoke of - the child or his father - and I did not feel the compulsion to care.

"Let's give him a name," she said this time. I swallowed a peg of spit, anticipating a surge of anger.

"Hand me the water. Is it cold?"

"Not as much," she made a face, "as you."

I took out my razor, my companion, my strength. Showing it to her, I spoke through my teeth, "This cold?" She passed the bottle. I predicted she would whistle, and she did. *I was soon soaked in a warm bathtub with Nina's hands scrubbing me from behind.* My realities were getting seamlessly integrated; it was almost too easy, too natural. I had to find a way for Zila to stop abusing my past to her advantage.

"Let's call him Chari," she went on whistling between words.

"Why Chari?"

"I heard you say the name when you were down at the hospital. I liked the sound of it. Must be short for?" she hoped for an answer.

"Don't remember. He died in the drain. Fell and died. He had a polio leg and could not come out. The rains fell hard that day." *I liked the soapy waters around my chest, making me want to tell the whole story in detail.* "He was my friend."

"You had friends?" Zila seemed more shocked than surprised.

"Only he. He too went away."

"That's bad. You were lonely."

"Not really. He burnt me in the laboratory - he and the others. But he started it. He thought laughing was a bloody joke."

Zila fumbled in the baby-bag.

"So I pushed him."

"Pushed him where?" she looked up awkwardly.

"In the drain," I told her the whole truth and nothing but the truth. "Yeah, let's name the kid Chari. I like it."

Bidiya sat under the tree on a cracked stone slab. Her silence reminded me of the lake in Didoli. Nina said it was a giant eye watching us, and I believed her. We would walk down the steep rocks to sit near the edge to watch the crabs bask in the sun of the hills. We had a favourite rock with a crack down the middle. I put my head in her lap while she told me stories without endings. Either she didn't know the end or wanted me to ask for more. I would just doze off bathed in her smell, and soaked in her sweat raining down on me. She didn't know which was a worse sin: waking me up or not wiping her brow. We did the cracked rock many times a week. And Bidiya sitting on something like it, looking forlorn so many hundred miles away made me feel wonderful. There was a quality unique to Bidiya which neither Daya nor Chanana possessed, though Zila did a bit. She was a real prostitute from the old school.

"You seem happy," Zila spoke in my ear. I smiled

at the morose gathering. Chanana sat surrounded by her dogs from the past. Some had been pups and some had languished in her absence. How they had a memory was a mystery to me, and then I remembered how my memory was a bitch that dogged me.

Zila held my hand. She was wearing Nina's smell deliberately loud to sway me, I could tell. She rubbed my back the way Nina would have. *I glowed inside in the warmth of the bathwater for the second time that evening.*

"While Chanana prepares the knives, you can hold this for me," she passed into my hands a little black stone that seemed familiar to me. *A wave of nausea pumped the glands under my tongue and bucketloads of saliva filled my jaw and dribbled down my chin.*

"Poor baby," Zila wiped the spit with her scarf. *I felt extreme grief welling up in my knotted gut. A teardrop streaked down my cheek.* Zila kept saying 'poor baby' and wiped my spit and tears alternately.

The baby began wailing on the stone altar where it had been placed naked. Chanana began chanting. The moon had risen in the east and the baby saw it and cried. I was sobbing quietly to myself. The women watched me through the haze of my eyes. Zila patted my hands. Chanana approached the baby, her knives glinting beautifully.

I began crying aloud, I remember. The knives, I remembered. *I saw Nina dead before me, her wrists spewing a red river. I believed the world had ended and I was left lonely. She looked at me with her sad smiling eyes that plucked at the feathers of my heart. I am going, she seemed to say, and I will never ever come back. What will you do without me? Who will stepmother you? Come near me and let me soak every bit of you into my memory.*

I was crying aloud. The baby was wailing louder. Chanana chanted against the wind. Zila kept calling me 'poor baby, poor baby'. Bidiya whimpered on her stone slab. *Chanana rubbed the knives together as she approached Nina. I howled towards the sky.*

"Do you want to sacrifice?" Zila asked me. I cried louder. "Do you want the baby to die? Do you want the sacrifice? Do you not want to take your words back? Uncle, do you want the knife to stop?"

*I saw Nina bleeding madly, I wanted her back. I held her hand and opened her palm. A little black stone fell out of it.*

"Do you want to stop the sacrifice, Uncle, do you want to stop it?" Zila shouted above the din. Chanana brought the knife close to the baby's neck.

"I don't want it," I cried, "just let the bleeding stop. I want her back as it was. I want Nina back. Just stop it. Please stop it." The stone rolled out of my hand. It was Nina's stone - she kept it close to her. She enjoyed its smoothness, it made her calm. I had told Zila about it in Didoli; I suspect she had found it in the house.

Zila said, "Hold it, Bitch. Didn't you hear the

man?"

Chanana dropped the knife and sank down in the dust. Bidiya rushed to grab the baby. Daya sat down where she stood. The baby's noise died down. Bidiya was laughing and hugging Zila. Zila came over and put her arms around me. She sat like that holding me for ages.

"We can throw this away now," she picked up Nina's stone and chucked it at the dogs.

My eyes were dry once again. A betrayal sat on my head. I knew Zila gave me the stone with such a specific purpose, and then just discarded it without any. She had played with my tears for Nina. She was still playing with my ears, fondling my head.

I looked around at the small family gathering. They were all smiling, laughing and throwing the baby in the air and catching it. Chanana clasped Bidiya as a mother would a daughter. Daya made stupid noises to the child. The dogs whined at the turn of their fate. It was inhuman to deny them blood after showing them the knives and the goat. I had to make amends for the folly of my family.

I took out my razor and sliced open Zila's neck.

While the three witches piled wood over Zila's corpse, I sat in the truck resting my head on the window and watched a tiny part of my past go gently past, bringing a smile within the confines of my beard.

I thought back to our beginning, thought back to Zila - fresh in her acid-burnt face, fresh in her Ninaness - during those first few weeks. Once, I had awoken to her casting a shadow on the early winter morning sunshine streaming through the bedroom window. She held my tea on a tray that turned out to be the kitchen mirror. Very few cooks hang mirrors in the kitchen, but she did in order to see her lesions heal painfully slow. As I sipped very thin tea, she held the mirror aloft. Had I been some softie husband, the kind they show on television, I would have choked, balked and demonstrated my displeasure in louder expressions. I merely took another sip.

"Nice work," I said, running my hand on my smooth left cheek. She had shaved off a large patch of my beard as I slept. During this time, three things happened: I was forced by Zila to shave completely, I wore a scarf covering my face as she did her veil, and we watched thirty movies in thirty days. You could say, in a way, that this was our honeymoon. Kamru knew nothing; he thought I was compensating for the acid-attack with this show of affection. He, too, began wearing a monkey-cap to be a part of the family.

I must admit, parting with the beard wasn't that bad. It made me invisible. Those who frequented the house wouldn't recognise me on the streets, even if I rubbed noses with them. I took Zila to all the pictures, sometimes two a night, until the bush grew back on - and with it, the old me - and made me look sterner.

Opposites attract - freedom and control always seem to get married, and maybe that's why no marriage is destined for an ever after. Zila was a tree hoping to take root and I, a rabbit looking for the hole in the wire-cage. Nina and I were fine. Zila and Kamru were fine. Anything else just wasn't right, wouldn't work.

When news of Zila's sacrifice carried itself to the city, only Kamru heard it. Only Kamru cried. I had not thought of it until then, but it was possible that Zila was Kamru's Nina. I had only loved her sweaty armpits and he saw the beauty in her facelessness. He could marry Bidiya only because he had no need to demonstrate his affection for Zila. I, too, was not married to Nina, I simply loved her.

We have been given elbows for one simple reason: to keep that distance. I think I have an electrical device in my elbow. It makes me stick them out, and it also inspires my hands to take up the razor when someone crosses the line. Zila came and sat too close to me and Zila tried to control me. I didn't slaughter her, it was my elbow.

I hoped the others got my greetings loud enough.

# *Chapter 35*

Business went on as usual. The famous singer enquired about Zila to be told that she had moved on and become someone else. But my memory was stalking me, tiring me out. I did not let the bitches too near except on sanitized occasions. I realized what Zila had figured out years ago. My memories jumped out at me from behind any sensation related to the past, and accosted me. I started plugging my ears and nose when the bitches were around. They had not yet discerned what was happening, but I suffered my memory nonetheless. I tried not to touch things I hadn't tested before for traces of history.

I moved out of the room at the house, that contained so much of Zila, to a small hall at the temple. Driving the truck meant I would have her memories sitting there dictating the day's agenda. The bitches managed the house and raised Chari.

I had gone to the prison to meet Kamru and buy my peace for having silenced his only friend. Bidiya was already there, showing off the baby - something Kamru was only fifteen percent interested in. Seeing me, his infatuation dipped to not more than five percent. He dropped the kid in Bidiya's lap and got up to sniff around my periphery as in the past.

He sported a beard and, I noticed for the first time, he had clumps of grey in his leftover hair as well. On his hands and feet were bandages of a yellowish tone from being washed and reused.

"I'm still your dog, Boss," he said as a greeting.

"What happened to your paws?" They did look like paws.

"Oh nothing, Boss, got lonely." The jail-people had sent word saying that my friend had taken just any object sharp enough and drawn blood. On being asked why, he merely smiled. So all things he could hurt himself with were exiled and the brave man went ahead, and used his teeth. It was only when someone came visiting were his shackles and muzzle removed.

"Zila's gone, what's the use," I said. The dog looked at me and hardly nodded. In his eyes was the deepest of solitudes, reminding me of the lake in Didoli. I felt nice and warm suddenly, and put my hands around his shoulders. Kamru's bones clutched at my fingers.

"You are not eating? How will you live?" I rubbed his back. He just looked up into my face as if waiting for a morsel. The skin around his eyes had loosened like a well-slept-in sheet. His nose held a drop at the tip. He wiped it with the back of his bandaged hand.

"Do you want to die?" I asked him in his ear. He nodded and as if his head was full of water, some poured out of his eyes and nostrils. I did not know Kamru could cry. Bidiya watched from a distance with eyes of uncertainty, and hands full of Chanana's unkept promise. I placed my back between her and Kamru.

"Take this," I slipped him my razor. His pupils shone as a child's. He hopped away without a word or a glance at either of us; I guess to hide the bone he had just discovered. Bidiya came up to me.

"He asked me to give you this," she handed me a tin box that belonged to a brand of assorted biscuits many years ago. It was partly rusted and partly dirty from having been handled after meals with unwashed hands on many an occasion. I tried the lid, it needed a coin. Bidiya gave me a bent spoon to flip it open. She was more curious to see what I saw. Her eyes were not on the box, but on my eyes. I took myself away to a far bench.

The lid came off easy with the spoon. From the box I pulled out a crumpled piece of newspaper. I unfolded it carefully on my lap and held up a black bit of wood wearing a cheap ring. I was holding between my fingers Nina's finger that went missing at the funeral. I remembered Kamru too, missing at Nina's funeral and more recently - the connection - the picture I had found of her living inside his dirty coat pocket. I wanted to rush back and ask him the meaning of all this before he escaped forever with his secret. I got the feeling Kamru owned just that much of Nina's affection as much as I owned Zila's.

In some ways, Nina was always mine and Zila was always Kamru's. But strangely enough, Kamru also needed Nina in the same way I needed Zila - fleetingly. When Nina died, that ephemeral love Kamru felt for her died too but he needed something to remember her by, something tangible, something only he could have. He liked to lop off fingers, that much I knew, but this wasn't the parting gift I had expected from him. It scratched the scab on my heart. Kamru was absent at Nina's funeral because he had taken her finger, and whatever emotions he felt for her, with him.

I held Nina's dead digit tighter in my grasp.

*The world spun around as a circus horse. I smelt the smoke of burning pinewood. Only three forms stood around the burning logs. A eunuch performed the dance of death. His liquor-breath overpowered the air, mixing with the smoke from the fire. Beneath the wood lay Nina with only nine fingers, slowly becoming ash. My tears turned into a howl. I beat my chest and the other man - Sattu - beat the drum. Kamru was nowhere to be found.*

Somewhere in the dark a man's voice demanded, "Who came to meet Kamru?" I opened my eyes to a small crowd gathered around me. My shirt was off, and my jute suit gathered at the waist. A pain hammered my head. I saw Bidiya bending over me in a flustered expression.

She half-cried and half-laughed, "The moron killed himself, I'm free. The moron killed himself, I'm free." I only half-heard her. *I could feel feet stomping on my chest and laughing. I covered my face with my hands before they peed on me.*

I woke up dead on Chanana's bed. The bitches sat on chairs white as ghosts in cheap movies.

"Don't tell him yet the dog just died," said Daya in an over-protective mood. I prayed to be saved from their goodness. In the evening when the prison invited me to take possession of Kamru's body, I asked for the razor too. I wanted to make peace with the fiend that killed my friend, I said. I shaved Chari's head with it because his own father had left him fatherless, defining his life. The way Nina had left me, rudderless. The true story of the finger now hung like a secret between the dead and me.

Nobody heard chanana's sob explode.

# Chapter 36

Things returned to normal. I went back to the house just to keep an eye on the minds of the three women now, when Zila too had gone Emarti's way. Something told me, I had to go gather together the devotees of Ooee on a day exactly one year away from Kamru's passing on. It was to be a celebration of freedom from every little sensation known to every emotion. A vision had descended upon me, so they said, behind the great idol just out of the blue. News flew around of Ooee having appeared at the base of my bed twice on a certain night when the wind blew in a perfect eight.

"This is the day," she had sat there talking in the likeness of Emarti, so the story went, "when you will tell them to collect, for on this day will they see me in your image."

"But why?" I was supposed to have enquired rather stupidly. "Why must you come down on that day?"

To which Ooee laughed and disappeared. I

went back to sleep with my head on my folded arms. Somewhere around three in the morning, when it was still night, I was woken up by a random shaking of my entire being. My body rose in the air and I remained suspended six feet above the ground in the upright position till the sun prepared to appear.

The next morning I had an answer to 'why'.

"That will be the day all wishes will be fulfilled. The greatest pleasures will rain down on those present, precisely at midnight," I recounted, but the mechanics of how this would happen were still not divulged to me. I had become the daily voice recorder of Ooee, and a visitation from her was now a matter of my entering the room behind the idol and emerging from it after an hour of meditation, it was presumed. No one enquired why my breath had a fermented flavour. Believers believe, bastards question.

My sessions were replaced by pronouncements.

I spent more time catching up on sleep. The bitches maintained decorum in the temple, and all other properties Ooee had acquired. Daya had the duties of managing the diversified business interests to keep her away from thinking on matters metaphysical. Chanana spread my word and a lot of gossip masquerading as miracles only she seemed to have witnessed. And Bidiya had the sole responsibility of raising Chari, out of my earshot and far from the reach of my eager razor.

Someone had calculated my age to exceed hundred by two decades. Some fine mathematician. I neither denied nor accepted any reports of any kind. I became like a legend, my exaggerated stories procreated on their own. My silence and bursts of revelation became matters of convenience for me.

I will never forgive Chanana for this. She spoke of the miraculous powers of the hair on my head and how hanging a strand around one's private parts would ensure a progeny endowed with Ooee's blessings. Had I not found a supplier of coir mats to meet the demand, I would have lost the use of my wooden comb. I had begun merely as Ooee's messenger, but now seemed to have somehow surpassed her fame.

To take it even further, my urine was dutifully collected in silver urns, and sealed in glass vials to be distributed at the current price of ten grams of gold. I wasn't surprised when Daya insisted on my surviving on a liquid diet as prescribed by a doctor of dubious intent. I showed Daya the razor I had managed to get back from police records, and she forgot to make the suggestion again.

Bidiya, however, continued to surprise me with her complete absence of any ambition. She did inspect the construction of the giant stage for the great event. An idol of no small proportions had been commissioned at a phenomenal payment equivalent to half a tonne of gold that would be in the form of vials of urine. Thus, I was advised by simple economics to drink more juice. Life had come full circle. No one begins by being famous and rich. I was where I was for the simple truth that I could spray urine at a roadside bougainvillea. I had achieved a monstrous following because my penis got caught in my zipper ten years ago. I had to thank an ugly girl with smelly armpits for showing me the way.

One day a young woman, in the congregation that I had begun addressing because of the numbers, asked me out of turn, "I want to marry you. What must I do?" I always propagated freedom, so anyone feeling annoyed at the sudden query had no reason to be. Jealousy, on the other hand, was an expression of freedom too and had no business to be curbed.

I smiled, and retired to my room at the temple to speak to the all-knowing Goddess. The entire audience waited for my return with a word from Ooee. I forgot to come back as I had dozed off on my gold and lacquer cot. And when I did emerge hours later, not a single soul had left her composure; I was pleased. I took my seat and began.

"I had been married till few months ago. Ooee instructs me now to take a wife on the great day when pleasure rains down from above. However, I must decline the hand of the remarkable lady who displayed the highest level of freedom, because my bride has already been chosen by HER. My bride brings pleasure no mortal can equal."

A growing murmur came like bees, and I waited for it to pass as masses cannot sustain surprise beyond a point. They are followers and had to start looking for a leader to take over the general drift of feelings. The lady of audacity stood up once again.

"Who is this divine mystery?" she laughed. Obviously, all she wanted was quick publicity, but I did her a bigger favour.

I said, "She shall be revealed on the great day and shall bring with her the greatest of pleasures. But Ooee wants you," I pointed my gaze at her of the brave questions, "to be the spirit of this grand celebration which we shall now call the 'Hahahohee'." I had thought of this one just then inspired by the woman's laugh. She couldn't believe her bleeding petticoat. "And what be your name, you newly-appointed keeper of the festival?"

She barely stammered something about being too overwhelmed by the honour, and I had to cut her short, "Your name?"

"Nina," she said quickly. I saw my twenty fingers curl inwards. I don't believe in miracles, I'm only known to perform them, yet here somebody had pulled a haunted mansion out of a hat. I was stunned, struck dumb. I think the world spun for a minute too many. I heard the thin note of a clarinet say, "I am Nina. I really am." The new keeper of Hahahohee was holding my hand delicately to her breast. My fingers closed upon her and she sighed. Then alarmed, she looked down.

"I'm bleeding," she announced to the crowds, "and it's not even my day." Four thousand or more women yelled and clapped. I had apparently performed another miracle. The new Nina was a natural: a total liar, a snake.

She moved in with us. And as becomes woman nature, the other inmates of the house unwelcomed her, partly for her younger skin and mainly because she said things to Chari which only I held the right to say. She called him a whore's dog. I found the coincidence confounding - first another Nina and now another dog. We were living in a world of instant miracles, I observed.

"Uncle," Bidiya woke me from one of my usual snoozes, "I must show you something." She expected me to protest, so she was ready, "I want to open your eyes." I told her I was wide awake, it was her eyes that needed examining. She glared at me disbelievingly and broke down. I wanted to pat her neck and strangle her right there.

"Just because her name is Nina doesn't make her Nina. Don't you see she is here to squeeze you," she wept.

"And why are you here, Bitch, to suckle?"

"We go a long way, Uncle. Look what she did." Bidiya rolled up her clothes revealing a pigeon tattoo on her inner thigh.

"How did she get that there?" I exclaimed. "She's good."

"Her pendant." I waited for a better explanation. "She hung it over the kitchen flame. Then she pushed me to the floor and put it there."

"Who knows about this?"

"You," Bidiya lowered her voice and went back to weeping. I was losing my happy disposition with all the emotional secretions.

"Where's your pup?" I enquired.

"Sleeping."

"All alone?" The look on her face changed from watching a family drama to cheap horror. She rushed out. I lay back feeling satisfied about the way New Nina was evolving as a keeper. She had followed instructions to a beautiful conclusion. As a small test, the kind I test trust with, I had told her to brand Bidiya, but she chose the spot and shape. And the most convincing part was she never bragged about it. Yeah, she was not your ordinary doggess, she went deeper and, therefore, higher. She had taken a risk and won. I reminded myself to watch her more carefully.

The day after the branding of Bidiya, we were imbibing tea when New Nina lifted a strand of her gossamer hair and put it behind her ears. Had it not been for those two particular seconds, I may have been fooled. In those two seconds she glanced at Bidiya and their eyes smiled knowingly, as if sharing a dirty secret.

I am a man in search of scruples, which means I tend to read entire books through just the small nuances in syntax. I find more truth in a woman's inaudible grunt than all her poised posturing. And every one of us is such a wonderful actor, so what people like me in positions of power have to do is, simply wait for the slip. This slip from grace is not a fall, it is a slight tremor in the calves that goes unnoticed. I dwell on these tremors because I believe they are generated in the rearing of a personality. When a very careful woman in elegant clothes skids an inch on a shiny marble floor, it is not an accident; it gives her away as an imposter. And women of class never slip.

Every moment is a photograph and one can't pose every second. My eyes were like cameras, clicking relentlessly, hoping to obtain the most truthful image at each moment. There is a lot to be learnt in the smaller seconds, which a lifetime may not divulge. In fact, seconds have saved my skin from vultures. Simply observing makes us astrologers.

Sometimes words too come in these smaller notations. I listen for sounds embedded in them. They contain Daya's cunning, Chanana's rage and Bidiya's sloppy slurping at my heels. The only sounds I can never read are the ones Chari makes, and they place him higher and therefore, in a position of danger to me. I am extremely wary of what a baby may be plotting. This New Nina was no baby. Two seconds of tossing her hair gave her away.

Some people are death-managers, some are killers, and some are just downright vampires - they thrive on pleasure. New Nina was so bloody perfect that she became a doubt I wanted out in the open. "Your name isn't Nina," my words caught her smack on the ear. She burned a bit and continued examining the weed filling a crack in the concrete. "Don't make me repeat myself."

She faced me, stoically. I liked the way she put her hand on my shoulder and said with a quiet severity, "How does it matter, Uncle?"

"If it doesn't, why are you that?"

She remained more quiet than calm now. I took her hand off me and caught her arm rather firmly to make myself more audible.

"You want to marry me, don't you? What for? What pleasures do I explode in your clever brain? You have the guts to get up in the middle of the congregation and be heard. You possess the name I'd never miss. You do such things, and you don't follow. I have worked with the blind and now I lead the blind, and I'm certain you are not one of them. You are not a follower, you are me." I said this to disarm her.

Now she let her guard down and smiled. This was no ordinary smile of a devotee, it was a conversation with an equal. She was the sum of the other three. "I still want to marry you," she said quite firmly.

"To kill me?"

"No," she said, "to wait for you to die."

"You don't want my business to die, do you?"

"That's why you must marry me."

"I am about to announce my mistress on the festival night."

"That could be me," she was so sure. It is so easy building an empire, yet so impossible finding a prince.

"Of course, it could very well be. Ooee can change her mind."

"Phooey," her disdain passed through her clenched teeth. Only a follower is a believer. A believer cannot lead. A leader stands away from his emotions and dictates. This creature who wanted to be called Nina deserved to be her more than any I had encountered. It seemed I had almost reached the end of my search although there were still some tests to be conducted. Two seconds of tossing her hair would cost her. A likeness of Nina or not, she would have to prove her worth like everyone else.

"I want you to perform."

"Already am, Uncle, already am."

"A miracle," I added.

She was left a step behind. "Isn't that too easy?" she mulled.

"Make Chanana chop off her ear with her own

hand." If she was the sum of the other three, she deserved to be tested three times more.

"You made me brand Bidiya."

"And make Daya throw the pup into the drain from the terrace," I said flatly. I watched her skin for signs of newly-formed lines betraying any feeling, and there were none. Either she was a great actor or supremely detached. "They must do this on their own without any help from you," I was stern this time, hinting subtly at my knowledge of their potential collaboration.

"Will do," she raised a military salute. "Must the whore's dog drown too?"

"It's your miracle, you decide. And remember, I'm the audience." I turned about at once and started walking away. She hastened to get inside the house. Things were going fine, I guessed. I hadn't still lost my touch.

I said a lot of stuff for a busy man. What I held back was a bit of derivation. Even a blind man can figure out how a woman happened to get so close to me so soon. New Nina had obviously been trained and planted in my house by the three bitches. Not even the worst whore will ever let another woman brand her there, let alone throw her kid in muck. There was quite a bit at stake here. If New Nina managed the miracles, she had definitely been planted. I was amazed at their ability to keep my life interesting.

Chanana got rid of her worthless hanging piece of ear without a whimper and Daya chucked the baby in the swirling drain without qualm. Bidiya dived in as a mother would, and emerged from the goo happier than ever.

New Nina stood at my elbow waiting for applause. My hand simply went to Mason's razor in my pocket and I held it out to her. "Get a golden one made. And four silver replicas."

She opened her mouth, my eyes told her to disappear. She may have been the keeper of Hahahohee, but to me she was just another perpetrator of pleasure. Once again my intuition was exact. New Nina had been planted by the three weird sisters.

I was alone.

# *Chapter 37*

We cut down to a diet of liquor and laughter, four months from the show. Close observers did say this was suicidal for a business with such growth prospects. To which I raised a glass and laughed. New Nina laughed and the three bitches laughed loudest. And when the sound of our glee went out, the throngs rolled. Very often, as a result, rain came down in torrents or the sun bore down its splendour, and the laughter grew wilder than the minds of women in the throes of jealousy. I went out to the masses one day with a happy announcement. "Yes, that is the day," I stood onstage and repeated myself again and again.

"That is the day," New Nina echoed theatrically. The crowds roared and cheered. The bitches, particularly Bidiya, stayed at home and drank themselves happy. The baby, always sleeping or smiling, no longer wanted to be weaned.

"Who will descend and set our worries free? What will she give us? " The crowd made a great noise. "Yes, the greatest of pleasures. Yes. Yes. Yes."

New Nina repeated the yesses in so much excitement that it was close to orgasmic. The women clamoured even more.

"Do you go home and scream?"

They yelled 'yes'.

"Do you go home and draw a drop of your being?"

They all screamed 'yes'.

"Does your own blood scare you or tell you to paint everything around you red?"

New Nina prompted, "Paint the sorrows red."

The crowd went madly 'yes'.

I was already tired but the show must go on, so I said, "Have you tasted your own blood?"

They howled 'yes'.

"What does it taste like?"

New Nina shouted 'freedom'.

They went 'yes'.

"Is it not pleasure?"

The thousands of women were bouncing up and down, to a tune playing somewhere, yelling 'yes, yes, yes'.

"Go home and get drunk and scream your hearts out. There is no pleasure greater than the pleasure within you."

The multitudes went berserk. I went back to my room. New Nina continued the discourse without any preconceived thought. For a manager of the fest, she was a fast learner and clever with her words. She could have been dictating the recipe for roast papaya soup and the believers believed in unison.

I always came back having spoken with Ooee. I always had something new to divulge.

"Buy a razor like mine," I showed them one day, holding it up. It was gold and bejewelled. "It could be gold or steel, but it has to be precious. Precious means perfect."

New Nina showed off her silver razor, "Or a razor like mine. Shining and sharp."

"Keep it closest to you till the day we shall dance." The women jumped with joy. "Such is the will of Ooee." I left for the day in a din of happiness.

As I made my pronouncements on the dais each day, I sat on a throne with a very high back almost ten feet tall. Ooee's image adorned both sides and a volunteer continued dusting the glass faces throughout the day with a handled wig made of horse hair. My seat was all silk and gold and extremely uncomfortable, which made me run off to the chamber on the pretext of having a word with Ooee. Otherwise, I had my own chair with two large wheels since Kamru disappeared. New Nina would push me around on it in what I suspected were expressions of impatience and disgust.

The memories had become more frequent and very easily triggered. Before an appearance, I would take an hour to meditate and push every sight and sound, and touch, and taste, and smell out of my mind. I wore gloves and earplugs. Camphor burned constantly in a small container attached to my jute robe because it was one odour that gave me space. And I was forever chewing a kind of medicinal root with no feelings attached.

Once back in my hole, they just piled on to me. Mother, Father, Zila, some random women I forget the connection to, and hundreds of babies crawling all over me. They pushed my wheelchair around the room making me very giddy and nauseous. My Nina sat on the bed mostly, unconcerned. Sometimes, I talked to her when I was sure no one would interrupt.

*"Are you comfortable, Nina?" I tried to get her to talk. She would mostly answer in hmmms. "I know there's another Nina, but I know she's not Nina. She's a witch."*

*"You like witches, don't you," Nina lifted her eyes. Her smell invaded the room with warmth.*

*"And you were the perfect one," Father butted in.*

*"Will you leave us alone, Father. Just shut your mouth," I had to tell him he was dead and of no use to anyone.*

*"Poor frustrated bugger," Nina tch-tched. "He was the lowest animal on Lower Lane. The scummiest, you know."*

*I pointed to Mother standing at the door in her bathrobe, "The scummiest one I know scared the workers away. Why didn't these two get along and leave the world alone? Eh, Nina?" She hadn't been listening to me and I felt bad.*

*"You were especially kind to Kamru," she said at last. I nodded. "He was a very important person, you know, and a very impotent one?"*

*"What do you mean, Nina? He has a son."*

*Nina shrugged her shoulder, "He just wasn't there. How would I know, you wonder? I know such a lot. He was just not there." She began giggling like a schoolgirl. I felt worse.*

*"But his son? Don't say even this one is mine." Nina started laughing real loud. I hadn't seen her so happy ever.*

*"I got you, didn't I?" she joked, "Should have seen your face. I was just pulling your puny little thing." She rolled on the bed.*

When your memories start making fun of you, I realized, you must shut yourself in a room and burn a lot of camphor. New Nina often found me suffocating and smelling good.

I had much drunkenness at the house as the days to Hahahohee became scarcer. Four women whom I loathed from my core surrounded me with stories of my own weaknesses and their bravado. I drank slowly soaking in their angst borne out of suffering and greed. New Nina too laughed louder, but consumed little. She was destined to find me dead one day and lead. Sometimes my transport and seat shook in an invisible rage that brought a faint smile to New Nina's watchful lips. I heard their every word and spoke little. The gold razor was clenched tight in my fist.

"He's been a good manager, this Uncle of ours," Daya slurred. "Now look at him. What is bothering you, Uncle?" she yelled near my ear as if I'd gone deaf. "You've become a god. What more do you want?"

New Nina intervened slyly, "Let the man be."

"I know," said Daya again, "a razor remains a razor. I just asked what more can a man want? What is all this Hahahohee?" Everyone laughed this time including New Nina. "Why waste money even if it is just money. Ask him, Nina. Only you can get inside his silence."

Bidiya's pup made some sounds on the floor near my feet. I looked down and the eyes looked up. He gurgled like the plumbing gone bad. *I saw Kutti sitting on my lap, playing with my chin.*

*"Don't do that now," I told her gently, "let's see how soft these hands are."* I moved the chair closer to Chari's fingers and Bidiya jumped out of her skin. She grabbed the pup and rushed to a corner shaking all over.

"You want to know what more I want? I want to crush that hand under my wheel, and watch you throw emotions at me. Come here, you," I motioned to Daya with the tip of my finger.

"Take it easy, Uncle," Chanana got up, "she meant nothing."

I told Daya to come real close so I may tell her some truths about my plans. She hesitated and rose slowly.

"Stay away from him," Bidiya shouted, "he has his hand in his pocket."

Daya was more confident of the lot, and craftier. She put her cheeks to my cheeks and whispered in my ear, "You really need to cut my neck?"

No I didn't want to, she just forced me to. Daya lay thrashing on the floor. *Kutti kept playing piano on my chin.*

"Take me back to my room," I ordered New Nina. "And someone clean up this mess."

# Chapter 38

Hahahohee came stealthily upon us. The construction of the stage was magnificent. Ooee's idol reflected in the sun in an incomplete state because the sculptor was not too sure of such high payments being made once the event flew past. He was also not pleased with my inability to produce urine even though I was consuming good pints of alcohol. It did not bother me in the least. I knew of so many broken idols that won more respect than complete ones.

The day had arrived. I had woken up in the middle of the night and bathed. I wore my new jute robe adorned with golden thread, and waited for dawn to kill the dark. I did not drink.

A million tents had cropped up on the acres around the temple. Some more elaborate than others. The large field had been cleared of any vegetation and white carpets spread to welcome a phenomenon - the greatest pleasure on Earth.

It would all begin at ten in the night. Large

lights like monster eyes stared at the dazzling carpet. There was so much movement inside the gates, yet not a soul outside was aware, I imagined. Fifty thousand women were expected to assemble.

I watched the operations from my wheelchair parked high near the dome of the temple. New Nina stayed behind me, anxious and important. She hadn't yet put on her robes, which were more resplendent than my rags.

"This is it then, Nina," I felt stronger.

"I believe in you, Uncle." Her belief had been fortified with conviction after Daya's disaster. She no longer grimaced at pushing my chair.

"You know what's most important."

"Yes, Uncle." She looked out over my head at some noise far away. "I think they are already celebrating in anticipation."

"Let them. This is an occasion to celebrate our freedom. How would you, under ordinary circumstances? What would you have succumbed to?"

"A man probably," she said with little shyness.

"There are no men out here if you've noticed," I laughed, "except the pup and I. And we are both not old enough."

She laughed too, though with sadness.

"You know, Uncle," she said wistfully, "I have grown fond of you. And I'm not saying this for the estate."

"Keep your emotions to yourself," I was stern. "Don't rub cheeks with me. The only person I care about will be there tonight. And you can't be as pleasurable as her."

"Try me."

I just laughed and asked her to push harder and not play around with my feelings.

"They are here," she informed me. Bidiya, Chanana and the pest emerged from a hole in the wall.

"Where's," and I stopped, having just remembered Daya's spirit had resigned from the daily grind, "the best place to sacrifice on the estate?"

All eyes looked at Chanana and she looked blank. She hadn't been paying attention, I guessed, so I repeated myself with some effort bordering on anxiety.

"The event is six hours away, I desire better tuning. Leave your thoughts under the staircase at the house and give me quick answers." Chanana nodded, Bidiya gawked, Chari bawled. "Tell me the exact place on the estate for a sacrifice. The best place inside or outside. If it's on a tree, tell me." We looked up at the sun by habit to ascertain the direction. Chanana held a scarf to the wind. We all watched her walk over to the edge of the dome and look out across the fields.

"Too many people out there," she said.

"Does it affect the outcome?" I enquired.

"No."

"Then shut up and work. The best place could be six feet under a rock, I'm fine with that. Just tell me quick."

New Nina placed a hand on my shoulder to calm me. I didn't like the display of intimacy in public. A sharp quiver at the collarbone told her so. She bit her lips. I could sense her rising anxiety by the waves travelling through her hands to the back of the chair. I saw Bidiya holding the pup tighter than usual.

I caught her eye, "He is safe. By the way you are holding him, he won't be very soon. I want him to suffer life as he has cheated death once. I want him to suffer life. What's wrong with this woman? Has she lost her bearing?" They all glanced at Chanana lying face down on the parapet. We all laughed, especially Bidiya who had rivers down her cheeks. I was properly packed in my armour and chewed furiously at the root. Any emotion was totally undesirable; a grand event was upon us - there was work to be done and no time for tears.

"It could be you we'll sacrifice," I told Bidiya and she stopped the taps instantly. She wiped her cheeks hurriedly, and began rocking the pup violently to stop the noise he made.

Chanana stood before me.

"Well go on," I snapped.

"There are two spots," she started.

"I said tell me the best," I screamed.

"You'll be surprised."

"Is this woman insane?" New Nina gestured for her to spit it out and be done with. The kid had started howling again. Bidiya tried to muffle him, and he cried louder. I was getting tired.

Chanana pointed to my crotch, "This place where we stand is the best. Just a little to the right." Her finger went like the needle on a compass, and came to rest behind Bidiya.

"Here? The top of the dome? Are we in some crazy movie or what? The top of the dome is the best you could think of?"

"Yes," she said with conviction and I was happy. I liked confidence.

"I will personally officiate the sacrifice. You have to meet me here both of you. And I need a goat." This sort of shocked them a bit. They looked at each other.

"Get a goat with curled horns carrying a baby." Now they relaxed somewhat. "Why are we looking so glum?" I clapped my hands. "Cheer up, Bitches, I'm getting married tonight."

Liquor and razors rained at the camp. I had given clear instructions to close the estate gates at nine. The volunteers, handpicked down the year, ensured no one slipped in or out. The revellers started staggering towards the white carpet. There were brawls broken up by mad laughter. New Nina had changed to a peacock-inspired attire and wore a tall headdress with feathers for effect. We watched the gathering storm.

The sacrificial spot on the dome was ready and the goat, as desired, chewed and shat intermittently. Chanana was dressed for the wedding, while Bidiya was made up as if it were her own. They were asked to stay put and keep an eye on the goat. Actually, the goat would keep them from wandering off into the heat of the actual event. The planning of the sacrifice was redundant and not important; it was merely for their royal distraction. Kamru's mother, Kamru's wife and Kamru's son were not invited to the party. For reasons of the heart, unwilling to be admitted by me, I felt the need to preserve the remainder of my faithful dog's family from what I knew could be their end.

"Let's go," I told New Nina. I could hear the gates close. She pushed me firmly towards the dark cloud of people. Fifty thousand women gathered to experience the greatest pleasure in the world.

A rumble went up as I rolled on to the stage. I lifted up both hands to acknowledge my supremacy over ordinary seekers of pleasure. The crowd growled in satisfaction. I let New Nina help me on my throne. Some stand-by volunteers rushed to the stage and took my arms. I gave them silver razors each, and they kissed my hands in rapture. And when the two young women raised the gifts for all to see, a roar of envy arose in certain corners. New Nina, too, showed off her elaborately decorated arms to silence them. It took a while before I could speak.

"Bitches," I began. Laughter and clapping ensued. I waited for the clamour to die down. I did not want to exhaust myself with two hours to kill.

"Bitches," I said without fanfare, "how many of you are bleeding right now? How many of you?" Too many hands went up with a glorious 'yeah, yeah, yeah'.

So I continued, "But I say every one of you is bleeding tonight. Every single womb of you."

"Every single woman here is bleeding tonight. Is it true or not?" New Nina laid emphasis as she was trained to. There was a sound of something close to a waterfall tumbling down from a thousand feet. Every single woman out there yelled her guts out. I smiled at New Nina, the night had begun well. I sipped from a glass.

"Where are your bottles? Where is your freedom? Where is your freedom in a bottle? The freedom that loosens your tongues! Let me see them." More noise. A total cacophony. New Nina raised a bottle to her lips and took a huge gulp. The crowd said 'cheers, cheers, cheers'. Some wanted to climb up on the dais and were pushed off by the volunteers. A scuffle broke out here and there, and we waited for the effect to abate once more.

"We are waiting," I said. There was silence. "We are waiting for the greatest pleasure tonight. But is this how we wait? What separates us from the herd? What gives us pleasure?"

The silence lingered; and I let it before I said in a hushed voice, "Our bodies." There was screaming, so I went louder, "Why are we whispering. What separates us from the herd is our bodies. Our breasts."

"Our breasts", New Nina shouted. She even clutched her chest.

"Why?"

"Why breasts?" New Nina yelled.

"For motherhood?" asked I. "No. Motherhood is for a few months of our lives, breasts are designed for arousal. Breasts are forever."

"Breasts are forever," New Nina repeated amidst a din.

"Breasts are for pleasure," I said.

The crowd repeated, "Breasts are for pleasure."

"Then why hide them like displeasure?" I looked at New Nina. She met my gaze, doubtfully. I nodded. She pulled off her robes displaying her bobbing mounds of flesh. "Show them. Go show them."

I had never seen so many shirts and blouses and jackets in the air. I was certain things were going well. New Nina got a bit carried away and began dancing. The crowds went wild. I wasn't complaining. It gave me some good five minutes to catch my breath. Then I motioned New Nina to stop and with her the thousands stopped.

"In five minutes, we will experience the biggest pleasure on earth," this, I said in utter solemnity.

"The biggest brightest happiest pleasure in the world," added New Nina now on a high.

"The pleasure of squeezing a breast."

New Nina demonstrated it with an apt expression. The crowd followed and we heard an imitation of a mooing herd coming from a large barn.

"What is this great pleasure? What is this thing that gives us pleasure? We are strangulating our breasts and it gives us pleasure. Why?" I cried to the women ready to break down. I knew the time had come and I must break the news soon. "What gives us this immense pleasure?"

New Nina clutched her breasts and moaned. The women groaned with desire. The time had come.

"The pain," said I.

"The pain," said New Nina.

"The pain," said an explosion of voices.

I stood up and almost screamed, "It is the pain that gives us pleasure. It is the bleeding that gives us pleasure. It is the organ which bleeds that gives us the most pleasure…until now."

New Nina got it and followed the lead, "It is the organ which bleeds that gives us the most pleasure. Until now." The devotees were delirious with a spiritual awakening. The clamour went on and on and on. I raised my hands. Silence. Drunk silence.

"What gives us the greatest pain on earth will give us the greatest pleasure. What gives us the greatest pain?"

New Nina asked, "What indeed gives us the greatest pain?"

I took out my gold razor, "This."

Mimicking every move, New Nina took out her silver razor, "This."

Every woman out there took out her precious razor, "This."

"This is the greatest instrument of pleasure for those who have bled every day," I cried with passion.

New Nina was looking at me through her tears and fears. I was sure I had got it right. I brought my razor close to my wrist and bid her do the same. She stared at me.

"Every woman who has bled every day, has suffered everyday, will experience the biggest pleasure today - the pleasure from the pain will lead you to freedom. Freedom!" I nodded to New Nina and she hesitated.

I hobbled up to her and held her hands. Her left hand raised the silver razor and brought it down on her right wrist. A red fountain burst on stage. "Like this," I cried, "This is the greatest pleasure, is it not?"

"Yes, yes," New Nina screamed, consumed by her importance.

"Let your instruments slowly lead you to pleasure, you miserable sufferers of pain," I hollered, "this is all Ooee asks of you." Some woman near the dais proved to be a real follower. She sliced both wrists and moaned with joy. That did it.

Another did it. Another did it. The multitude did it. I bent down to watch New Nina writhe on the wooden planks. She was smiling.

"You've just married me," I said and sat down on my wheelchair, and rolled away towards the temple where two bitches and a goat awaited me. The vacuole in my heart was still there. "But I haven't married you," I added. The moaning and groaning followed me a great distance and then almost died.

I wasn't yet aroused.

# Chapter 39

I went to my chamber behind the idol. I had to lie down. My temples hammering the wall. Images of women slitting their wrists outside ran through my mind. Blood, all I saw was blood. My hands were shaking like insane. And the beat in my heart pounded on my ribs to no end.

*"Happy?" I heard Nina's voice. My Nina, not New Nina.* I closed my eyes tight wanting to shut out everything that very moment but, I had never been good at running away from the past. *I saw blood splattered on the white sheets.*

*"Happy to see so many do a Nina?" she said affectionately. I felt her palm on my hair, her smell all over me.* I felt good, yeah. I had expected to fall down and cry, but I was somewhat happy, though I wasn't yet aroused. I was indeed happy to see so many do a Nina - to mimic her pain, her pleasure, her sacrifice - but I wasn't satiated enough.

*"Look who's come to see you," Nina said this in a mocking way. I didn't have to open my eyes; I heard*

*Mother's wheezy breathing. She just sat down and, I think, framed her sentences with care. After all, the two had been married to the same man and a bit of comfort could not be dismissed.*

*Mother shifted on the bed and I expected her to come up with a curse. "You are taking revenge, aren't you? If all this noise makes you happy, well go ahead and be happy. At least I'll keep out of this. A few thousand women will die tonight, including someone's namesake, and a thousand will have cases of suicide against them. They will connect the earlier ones to you too. Perfect. By your distorted logic, I too should have slit my wrists tonight like someone we know." I didn't think it was important for me to answer her, and also I felt a sneeze coming on.*

*"Emarti," Nina informed me in a low voice. "Sorry about her. It was a bad idea. But you've made her a goddess or given a goddess a likeness of her. This is unfair to the rest of us, no?"*

*I turned on my side. Emarti's pineapple smell was beginning to bother me again. The camphor had long gone out and so had my chewy root or else I would have stuffed the root up my nose. I put my fingers deep in my ears. It rarely worked.*

*"You pimp," she came to the point. And that is all she said. I was aware of her communication abilities. I was tempted to ask if the knives still hurt and then decided against. Going by the pattern here, Zila was expected soon.*

*"Quite an assembly, eh Uncle," Nina emphasized the Uncle part. She had been pulling my leg too often recently. "How many more expected?" How was I to know, she was the organizer of the sit-in. Strangely, she was sitting quite out of my comfort. "Now who is this?"*

*I felt a hand on my shoulder. "That was awesome, Husband. Three hundred and five at last count."*

*Mother whistled. Emarti raised her eyebrows.*

*"The new Nina?" Nina wanted to clarify. I nodded softly.*

*"They have broken down the gate. The television guys are in. The authorities are looking for you. Just look out of the window, Husband. See the glittering red lights. We had a hit." I wanted to tell her that I had a hit and she was one of those hit. But Nina pinched me before I could; she knew me still. Her smell lingered harmlessly.*

I put the thumbs up my nose. Now the only thing to touch me was touch. *Zila failed to turn up and Daya probably still hadn't got over her shock.* I did feel something wet on my big toe. I thought it would go away, but it only got worse. The thing was sucking my toe and making sounds of contentment. I opened my eyes a chink and saw nobody. The sucking went on.

So I raised myself with great labour. A pair of eyes looked back at me as on another occasion.

"You son of a dog," I pulled my foot out of

Kamru's pup's mouth, "want your thing diced?" He gurgled something in a foreign tongue, mocking me. Bidiya had left him behind, as far away from the dome as possible and right into my arms. I fondled the razor in my pocket and straightened up, remembering suddenly.

"The dome. I must go to the dome."

I rose painfully from my gold and lacquer cot, anxious to get to the location of the sacrifice. Chanana and Bidiya would be waiting there. The wheelchair was nowhere to be found. I would have to walk up all the hundred or so steps - that stood close to my cot - to get to the roof of the temple. I started at the first step and sank down. The goat's bleats and the bitches' exclamations filtered down to me. I had to sacrifice; I had to feel blood on my hands. They were trembling, itching to kill.

I lay back on the stairs and reached inside my pocket for my golden instrument of pleasure. The greatest pleasure on earth. I smiled as I gradually unsheathed the blade. I had to manage with the second best place for sacrifice, eh Chanana? I couldn't test the blade on the goat anymore. What a waste. I brought the instrument to my wrist, prepared to be aroused one last time. The edge went just about inside my skin when a sound distracted me.

The pup sat teasing me from the base of my cot.

"Come here, pup," I whistled, "Come here, come here." It regarded me and said something funny that made it smile. It had a nice smooth neck. The razor in my hands cried out to feel that smoothness.

"Come here, you son of a dog."

Chari got down on all fours and came gurgling towards me. The noise from around hurtled towards me. The banging in my head became music. The shouts became beats. The cacophony became a symphony. The sound of chaos pleased me considerably.

Chaos. It was chaos, suddenly my whole being shivered. I looked away from the pup and into the distance; the golden razor fell from my hand. I had created a Goddess and destroyed her. I had raised a mammoth and crushed it. I had found success and adulation and killed it. I had brought peace and made it cry out. I had turned an empire into utter chaos.

It was chaos and not mere death that was the greatest pleasure of all. Pleasure wasn't painted with the red of blood; it was decorated with the sounds of anarchy, embellished with the uproar of orgasm, it was set against the backdrop of destruction. I had created the biggest pleasure, Nina. I had created chaos. I clenched my fists and breathed hard.

I was aroused.

# *Chapter 40*

I am a seventy-year old pimp.

Bend a little closer and I'll tell you what happened after.

Shashank Gupta means *'Moon Secret'*. His mother thought naming her very dark third-born so would mysteriously lighten his complexion. This has not happened in 49 years. Instead, his career has waxed and waned like the moon.

After attending boarding school in a beautiful hill-town, he learnt to look at the workers on his father's farm with utter disdain, but want of good grades pushed him to horticulture. Two months into his PhD, he revolted and bolted, choosing to work on the blessed farm. And then 6 years of growing-cutting-growing crops and the bleak prospects of gentlemen farmers in India, made him run away to Mumbai at 29.

He went on to become a copywriter in advertising at the very bottom of the ladder and took 7 years and some terrible campaigns to be called a Creative Director.

LITERARY

ISBN 978-81-8386-130-4

₹325 $11.99 £9.99

tara
India Research Press
www.indiaresearchpress.com

Cover design and illustration
by **Shilpa Shanker Narain**